A TASTE OF THE COUNTRY

Editors: Linda Piepenbrink, Nancy Mack
Food Editor: Mary Beth Jung
Assistant Editors: Sandy Trzesniewski, Patty Kishpaugh
Art Director: Ellen Lloyd
Cover Design and Illustrations: Jim Sibilski
Food Photography: Mike Huibregtse, Judy Anderson
Directors of Food Photography: Peter Loomans, Judy Larson,
Sue Myers, Linda Dzik, Peggy Bjorkman
Test Kitchen Assistant: Denise Simeth

©1993, Reiman Publications, L.P.
5400 S. 60th St., Greendale WI 53129
International Standard Book Number: 0-89821-105-0
Library of Congress Catalog Card Number: 93-84018

Recipes for dishes featured on front and back covers can be
found on pages 71 and 79; recipes for dishes shown above on page 25.

...in the country, appetites usually are brawny. And when they are, nothing satisfies better than hearty beef dishes!

But best of all—as you'll see here and on the following pages—beef also can break menu monotony...without doing the same to your budget.

From soups and stews to sandwiches and mouth-watering main courses (almost all calling for less-expensive cuts of meat), there are many months of imaginative and affordable eating in store for your family. So let the beef feast begin at your table today!

PRIME BEEF. Clockwise from lower left: **Old-World Sauerbraten** (p. 9), **Round Steak Stroganoff** (p. 9), **Snappy Barbecue Beef Sandwiches** (p. 9), **Hot Beef and Hazelnut Salad** (p. 9), **Oriental Beef and Cauliflower Stew** (p. 9), **Steak Soup** (p. 10), **Grilled Beef Kabobs** (p. 10), **Santa Fe Stew** (p. 10).

...w foods "stick to your ribs" like beef, and these delicious dishes are designed to do just that. Friends or family will be pleased to "meat" you at dinnertime when you ladle up bowls of Beef Stew with Cheddar Dumplings, serve savory Hungarian Short Ribs, offer easy-to-make Caraway Beef Roast or pass the Italian Beef Roll-Ups.

GRADE A! Clockwise from lower left: **Beef Stew with Cheddar Dumplings** (p. 10), **Hungarian Short Ribs** (p. 10), **Caraway Beef Roast** (p. 11), **Italian Beef Roll-Ups** (p. 11).

FOR A MEAL that's hearty in a hurry, try any of these delicious fast-to-fix beef dishes!

SPEEDY STROGANOFF

Jo-Ann Knicely, Midland, Ontario

- 2 tablespoons cooking oil
- 2 cups leftover cubed cooked roast beef
- 1 garlic clove, minced
- 1/3 cup chopped onion
- 2 tablespoons all-purpose flour
- 1 teaspoon salt
- 1/2 teaspoon paprika
- 1 can (10 ounces) mushroom stems and pieces, drained
- 1 can (10-3/4 ounces) cream of chicken soup, undiluted
- 1/2 cup water
- 1 cup (8 ounces) sour cream
- Cooked wide egg noodles
- Chopped fresh parsley

In a skillet, heat oil over medium-high. Saute beef, garlic and onion. When onion is tender, reduce heat to low; stir in flour, salt and paprika. Cook 5 minutes. Stir in mushrooms, soup and water. Simmer 10 minutes. Fold in sour cream; heat through but do not boil. Serve immediately over noodles. Garnish with parsley. **Yield:** 4-6 servings.

MUSTARD GRILLED STEAKS

Sharon Kraeger, Plattsmouth, Nebraska

- 1/3 cup Dijon mustard
- 1 tablespoon chopped fresh parsley
- 2 tablespoons honey
- 1 tablespoon cider vinegar
- 1 tablespoon water
- 1/4 teaspoon hot pepper sauce
- 1/8 teaspoon coarsely ground pepper
- 2 beef top loin steaks (1 inch thick)
- 1 large onion, cut into 4 thick slices

Combine the first seven ingredients. Brush over both sides of the steaks and onion slices. Grill over hot coals, turning once, 15-20 minutes or until steaks have reached desired doneness and onion is tender. Brush occasionally with sauce during grilling. Serve onion slices alongside each steak. **Yield:** 2 servings.

QUICK BEEF STEW

Valerie Cook, Hubbard, Iowa

- 2 cups leftover diced cooked roast beef
- 1 can (16 ounces) mixed vegetables, liquid drained and reserved
- 1 can (10-3/4 ounces) cream of celery soup, undiluted
- 1 can (10-3/4 ounces) cream of mushroom soup, undiluted
- 1/2 teaspoon dried thyme, optional
- 1/4 teaspoon dried rosemary, optional
- Pepper to taste

In a saucepan, combine beef, vegetables, soups and seasonings. Heat through. If desired, add the reserved vegetable liquid to thin the stew. **Yield:** 4 servings.

SESAME BEEF

Kim Champlin, Miami, Florida

- 1 pound sirloin steak, cut into 1/8-inch strips
- 2 tablespoons sugar
- 3 tablespoons cooking oil, *divided*
- 2 tablespoons soy sauce
- 1/4 teaspoon pepper
- 3 green onions, thinly sliced
- 2 garlic cloves, minced
- 1 tablespoon sesame seeds
- Rice *or* chow mein noodles

Place beef in a glass bowl. Combine sugar, 2 tablespoons oil, soy sauce, pepper, onions, garlic and sesame seeds. Pour over beef and toss to coat. Let stand 15 minutes. In skillet or wok, heat remaining oil over high heat; add beef and marinade. Stir-fry until beef is brown and has reached desired doneness. Serve immediately over rice or noodles. **Yield:** 4 servings.

ROAST BEEF WITH MUSHROOM SAUCE

Rev. Arthur Tiffen, Williamsfield, Ohio

- 2 tablespoons butter *or* margarine
- 3/4 cup thinly sliced onion
- 1/4 pound fresh mushrooms, sliced
- 2 tablespoons all-purpose flour
- 1/4 teaspoon ground marjoram
- 1/4 teaspoon garlic salt
- Salt and pepper to taste
- 3/4 cup beef broth
- 1/4 cup ketchup
- 8 slices leftover cooked roast beef

In a skillet, melt butter over medium heat. Saute onion for 5 minutes. Add mushrooms and saute 2-3 minutes. Stir in the flour and seasonings. Add broth and ketchup. Bring to a boil, stirring constantly. Reduce heat to low; simmer 10 minutes. Add beef and heat through. **Yield:** 4 servings.

PRONTO BEEF/ VEGETABLE SOUP

Dottie Casale, Ilion, New York

- 3 cups leftover cubed cooked roast beef
- 1 cup diced carrots
- 1 cup diced peeled potatoes
- 1 cup corn
- 1 cup cut green beans
- 1/2 cup chopped onion
- 1 quart tomato sauce
- 1/2 teaspoon salt
- 1 teaspoon dried basil
- 1 teaspoon dried oregano
- 1 tablespoon chopped fresh parsley

In a large saucepan, combine all ingredients. Bring to a boil; reduce heat and simmer 30 minutes or until vegetables are tender. If necessary, add 1/2 to 1 cup water to thin soup. **Yield:** 6-8 servings.

BOWL OVER family, friends with speedy soup (recipe above)—it's done beef-ore you know it!

E njoy a year-round harvest of good eating from your garden (and your grocer) with the recipes shown here. Loaded with vegetables, both the Summer's End Stew and Chicken and Okra Gumbo go nicely with freshly baked bread. Serve the lip-smacking Bacon-Stuffed Burgers with a generous helping of spicy Mission Baked Beans—all guaranteed to please hearty appetites!

GARDEN VARIETY. Clockwise from top: **Chicken and Okra Gumbo** (p. 11), **Summer's End Stew** (p. 11), **Bacon-Stuffed Burgers** (p. 12), **Mission Baked Beans** (p. 12).

OLD-WORLD SAUERBRATEN

Phyllis Berenson, Cincinnati, Ohio

(PICTURED ON PAGE 4)

- 2 tablespoons cooking oil
- 1 beef rump roast (5 to 6 pounds)
- 2 onions, sliced
- 1 cup vinegar
- 2 cups water
- 1/4 cup lemon juice
- 3 bay leaves
- 6 whole cloves
- 2 teaspoons salt
- 1/2 teaspoon pepper
- 4 to 5 tablespoons ketchup
- 12 gingersnaps, crumbled

In a Dutch oven, heat oil over medium-high. Brown beef on all sides. Add all remaining ingredients except gingersnaps; bring to a boil. Reduce heat; cover and simmer until beef is tender, about 3 hours. During the last 30 minutes, stir in gingersnaps. Remove meat; discard bay leaves and cloves. While slicing meat, bring gravy to a boil to reduce and thicken. **Yield:** 14-16 servings.

ROUND STEAK STROGANOFF

Brenda Read, Burns Lake, British Columbia

(PICTURED ON PAGE 4)

- 1/2 cup all-purpose flour
- 1 teaspoon salt
- 1/2 teaspoon pepper
- 1 teaspoon paprika
- 1-1/2 to 2 pounds round steak, trimmed and cut into thin strips
- 3 tablespoons butter *or* margarine
- 1 cup chopped onion
- 1 garlic clove, minced
- 1 can (10-1/2 ounces) condensed beef broth
- 1/2 teaspoon dry mustard
- 3 tablespoons chili sauce
- 1 pound fresh mushrooms, sliced
- 2 cups (16 ounces) sour cream
Cooked noodles
Chopped fresh parsley

Combine flour, salt, pepper and paprika in a plastic bag. Shake beef strips in bag until well coated. In a large skillet, melt butter over medium heat. Brown half the beef at a time. Remove. Add onion and garlic; cook until tender. Return beef to the skillet. Add broth, mustard, chili sauce and mushrooms; cover and simmer until the beef is tender, about 1 hour. Just before serving, stir in sour cream. Heat gently but do not boil. Serve immediately over noodles. Garnish with chopped parsley. **Yield:** 6-8 servings.

SNAPPY BARBECUE BEEF SANDWICHES

Patricia Throlson, Hawick, Minnesota

(PICTURED ON PAGE 4)

- 1 beef chuck roast (4 pounds)
- 1 cup ketchup
- 1 cup barbecue sauce
- 4 cups chopped celery
- 2 cups water
- 1 cup chopped onion
- 2 tablespoons vinegar
- 2 tablespoons brown sugar
- 2 tablespoons Worcestershire sauce
- 1 teaspoon chili powder
- 1 teaspoon garlic powder
- 1 teaspoon salt
Rolls *or* buns

Place beef in a Dutch oven. Combine all remaining ingredients except the rolls; pour over beef. Cover and bake at 350° for 5 hours, turning beef occasionally. Shred beef with a fork. Serve on rolls or buns. **Yield:** about 24 servings.

HOT BEEF AND HAZELNUT SALAD

Ruth Gooding, Los Angeles, California

(PICTURED ON PAGE 5)

✓ This tasty dish uses less sugar, salt and fat. Recipe includes *Diabetic Exchanges*.

- 1 pound sirloin steak, sliced across grain into thin strips
MARINADE:
- 1/4 cup sliced green onions
- 2 garlic cloves, minced
- 2 tablespoons light *or* regular soy sauce
- 1 tablespoon vegetable oil
- 1 tablespoon water
DRESSING:
- 2 tablespoons cider vinegar
- 2 tablespoons light *or* regular soy sauce
- 2 tablespoons vegetable oil
- 1 garlic clove, minced
- 1 teaspoon sugar
- 1/4 teaspoon curry powder
- 1/4 teaspoon ground ginger
- 8 to 10 cups torn salad greens
- 1/4 cup coarsely chopped hazelnuts, toasted

- Sliced green onions
- Chopped sweet red *or* green peppers

Place beef in a glass mixing bowl. Combine marinade ingredients; pour over beef. Allow to stand at room temperature 30 minutes. Meanwhile, combine dressing ingredients; set aside. Place greens in a large salad bowl; refrigerate. In a skillet over high heat, brown half the beef and marinade. Remove and then brown remaining beef. Drain and add all beef to greens. In the same skillet, heat dressing. Pour over salad and quickly toss. Top with hazelnuts, onions and peppers. Serve immediately. **Yield:** 4 servings. **Diabetic Exchanges:** One serving (using light soy sauce) equals 3-1/2 meat, 1 vegetable, 1 fat; also, 329 calories, 423 mg sodium, 70 mg cholesterol, 6 gm carbohydrate, 28 gm protein, 22 gm fat.

ORIENTAL BEEF AND CAULIFLOWER STEW

Deborah Cole, Wolf Creek, Oregon

(PICTURED ON PAGE 5)

✓ This tasty dish uses less sugar, salt and fat. Recipe includes *Diabetic Exchanges*.

- 2 tablespoons cooking oil
- 1-1/2 pounds lean round steak, cut into 1-inch cubes
- 3 cups beef broth
- 1 small head cauliflower, separated into florets
- 1 green pepper, cut into chunks
- 1/4 cup light *or* regular soy sauce
- 1 garlic clove, minced
- 1-1/2 teaspoons grated fresh gingerroot, optional
- 2 to 3 tablespoons cornstarch
- 1/2 teaspoon sugar
- 1/4 cup water
- 1 cup sliced green onions
Cooked rice

In a skillet, heat oil over medium-high. Brown meat on all sides. Add broth; cover and simmer until beef is tender, about 1 hour. Add cauliflower, green pepper, soy sauce, garlic, and gingerroot if desired. Cover and simmer until the vegetables are tender, about 5-7 minutes. Combine cornstarch, sugar and water. Stir into meat mixture. Bring to a boil, stirring constantly; cook 2 minutes or until thickened. Stir in green onions. Serve on rice. **Yield:** 6 servings. **Diabetic Exchanges:** One serving (using light soy sauce) equals 2-1/2 lean meat, 1 vegetable; also, 165 calories, 771 mg sodium, 82 mg cholesterol, 8 gm carbohydrate, 23 gm protein, 4 gm fat.

STEAK SOUP

Mary Dice, Chemainus, British Columbia

(PICTURED ON PAGE 5)

 This tasty dish uses less sugar, salt and fat. Recipe includes *Diabetic Exchanges*.

2 tablespoons butter *or* margarine
2 tablespoons cooking oil
1-1/2 to 2 pounds lean round steak, cut into 1/2-inch cubes
1/4 cup chopped onion
3 tablespoons all-purpose flour
1 tablespoon paprika
1 teaspoon salt, optional
1/4 teaspoon pepper
4 cups beef stock *or* broth
2 cups water
1 bay leaf
4 sprigs fresh parsley, chopped
2 sprigs celery leaves, chopped
1/2 teaspoon dried marjoram
1-1/2 cups cubed peeled potatoes
1-1/2 cups sliced carrots
1-1/2 cups chopped celery
1 can (6 ounces) tomato paste

In a Dutch oven, melt butter over medium heat; add oil. Brown beef and onion. Combine flour, paprika, salt and pepper; sprinkle over beef and mix well. Stir in stock and water. Add bay leaf, parsley, celery leaves and marjoram. Bring to a boil; reduce heat and simmer, covered, about 1 hour or until tender. Add potatoes, carrots and celery. Simmer, covered, for 30-45 minutes or until vegetables are tender and soup begins to thicken. Stir in tomato paste; simmer, uncovered, 15 minutes. Remove bay leaf before serving. **Yield:** 6 servings. **Diabetic Exchanges:** One serving (without added salt) equals 3-1/2 meat, 1 starch, 1 vegetable; also, 347 calories, 682 mg sodium, 93 mg cholesterol, 17 gm carbohydrate, 33 gm protein, 16 gm fat.

GRILLED BEEF KABOBS

Dolores Lueken, Ferdinand, Indiana

(PICTURED ON PAGE 5)

1 pound boneless sirloin steak, cut into 1-1/2-inch cubes
1 bottle (8 ounces) French *or* Russian salad dressing
2 tablespoons Worcestershire sauce
2 tablespoons lemon juice
1/8 teaspoon pepper
1/8 teaspoon garlic powder
8 to 10 bacon strips, cut in half
1 sweet red pepper, cut into chunks

1 green pepper, cut into chunks
2 small zucchini squash, cut into chunks
8 medium fresh mushrooms
1 large onion, quartered, optional

Place beef in a shallow glass pan. Combine salad dressing, Worcestershire sauce, lemon juice, pepper and garlic powder. Pour over beef. Cover and refrigerate 8-24 hours. Drain and reserve marinade. Wrap bacon around beef cubes. On metal or soaked wooden skewers, alternately thread beef and vegetables. Grill over hot coals for 10-15 minutes or until the desired doneness is reached. Baste frequently with marinade. **Yield:** 4 servings.

HUNGARIAN SHORT RIBS

Joanne ShewChuk
St. Benedict, Saskatchewan

(PICTURED ON PAGE 6)

2 to 3 tablespoons cooking oil
4 pounds short ribs with bones
2 medium onions, sliced
1 can (15 ounces) tomato sauce
2 cups water, *divided*
1/4 cup packed brown sugar
1/4 cup vinegar
1-1/2 teaspoons salt
1-1/2 teaspoons dry mustard
1-1/2 teaspoons Worcestershire sauce
1/4 teaspoon paprika
Cooked wide noodles

In a Dutch oven, heat oil over medium-high. Brown ribs on all sides. Add onions; cook until tender. Combine all remaining ingredients except noodles; pour over ribs. Reduce heat; cover and simmer until the meat is tender, about 3 hours. Thicken gravy if desired. Serve over noodles. **Yield:** 6-8 servings.

SANTA FE STEW

Patti Henson, Linden, Texas

(PICTURED ON PAGE 4)

2 tablespoons cooking oil
1 lean beef roast (about 2 to 3 pounds), cut into 1/2-inch cubes
2 medium onions, sliced
1 can (10 ounces) tomatoes with jalapenoes* *or* 1 can (16 ounces) tomatoes, cut up, liquid reserved
1 can (15 ounces) pinto beans, rinsed and drained
2 cans (4 ounces *each*) chopped green chilies

1 can (10-1/2 ounces) condensed beef broth
1 tablespoon sugar
1 garlic clove, minced
1 to 2 teaspoons ground cumin
1 green pepper, chopped
1 cup water
Salt to taste
Shredded Monterey Jack cheese

In a Dutch oven, heat oil over medium-high. Brown beef on all sides. Add all remaining ingredients except cheese; bring to a boil. Reduce heat; simmer 1-1/2 hours or until meat is tender. Serve in bowls topped with cheese. (*Look for tomatoes with jalapenoes in the ethnic food section of your grocery store.) **Yield:** 6-8 servings.

BEEF STEW WITH CHEDDAR DUMPLINGS

Jackie Riley, Garrettsville, Ohio

(PICTURED ON PAGE 6)

1/2 cup all-purpose flour
1/2 teaspoon salt
1/2 teaspoon pepper
2 to 3 pounds beef stew meat, cut into 1-inch pieces
2 tablespoons cooking oil
1/2 teaspoon onion salt
1/2 teaspoon garlic salt
1 tablespoon browning sauce
5 cups water
5 beef bouillon cubes
4 carrots, sliced
1 medium onion, cut into wedges
1 can (16 ounces) green beans, drained
DUMPLINGS:
2 cups buttermilk biscuit mix
1 cup (4 ounces) shredded cheddar cheese
2/3 cup milk

Combine flour, salt and pepper. Coat meat with flour mixture. In a Dutch oven, heat oil over medium-high. Brown meat on all sides. Add onion salt and garlic salt, browning sauce, water and bouillon. Bring to a boil; reduce heat and simmer, covered, about 1 hour. Add carrots and onion. Simmer, covered, until vegetables are tender. Stir in green beans. For dumplings, combine biscuit mix and cheese. Stir in enough milk to form a soft dough. Drop by tablespoonful into bubbling stew. Cover and simmer 12 minutes (do not lift cover) or until dumplings test done. Serve immediately. **Yield:** 6-8 servings.

> **STEW SECRET:** Add chopped turnip to beef stew for a delicious, slightly sweet taste.

CARAWAY BEEF ROAST
Beverly Swanson, Red Oak, Iowa

(PICTURED ON PAGE 6)

3 tablespoons cooking oil
1 beef rump *or* chuck roast (3 pounds)
1 cup hot water
1-1/2 teaspoons instant beef bouillon
1/4 cup ketchup
1 tablespoon Worcestershire sauce
1 tablespoon instant minced onion
1 teaspoon salt
1/2 teaspoon pepper
2 teaspoons caraway seeds
2 bay leaves
2 tablespoons all-purpose flour
1/4 cup water
Cooked potatoes and carrots, optional

In a Dutch oven, heat oil over medium-high. Brown roast on all sides. Drain. Combine water, bouillon, ketchup, Worcestershire sauce, onion, salt, pepper and caraway. Pour over roast. Add bay leaves. Cover and bake at 325° for 3 hours or until tender. Remove roast to a warm serving platter. Combine flour and water. Stir into pan juices. Bring to a boil, stirring constantly. Cook until thickened, adding additional water if necessary. Remove bay leaves. Serve with cooked potatoes and carrots if desired. **Yield:** about 12 servings.

ITALIAN BEEF ROLL-UPS
Lucia Johnson, Massena, New York

(PICTURED ON PAGE 6)

1-1/2 pounds thinly sliced round steak
Salt and pepper to taste
1 cup dry bread crumbs
1 cup grated Parmesan cheese
1/4 cup finely chopped fresh celery leaves
1 teaspoon dried parsley
1 teaspoon dried basil
1/2 teaspoon dried oregano
2 tablespoons vegetable *or* olive oil
4 cups spaghetti sauce
Cooked pasta

Pound meat to tenderize. Sprinkle with salt and pepper. Cut into 3-in. to 4-in. squares. Combine the bread crumbs, cheese, celery and herbs. Place a heaping spoonful of crumb mixture on each meat square and roll up. Secure with string or a toothpick. Roll meat in remaining crumb mixture. In a large skillet, heat oil over medium. Brown roll-ups on all sides. Pour spaghetti sauce over all; cover and simmer 1-1/2 hours or until meat is tender. Serve with pasta. **Yield:** about 6 servings.

SUMMER'S END STEW
Laura Garton, Lenox, Massachusetts

(PICTURED ON PAGE 8)

 This tasty dish uses less sugar, salt and fat. Recipe includes *Diabetic Exchanges*.

1-1/2 pounds beef stew meat, trimmed
1 tablespoon cooking oil
8 to 12 medium fresh tomatoes, peeled and cut up
2 cups tomato juice *or* water
2 medium onions, chopped
1 garlic clove, minced
1/2 teaspoon pepper
2 teaspoons salt, optional
4 to 6 medium potatoes, peeled and quartered
3 to 5 carrots, sliced
2 cups frozen corn
2 cups fresh cut green beans
2 cups frozen peas
2 to 3 celery stalks, sliced
1 cup sliced summer squash
1/4 cup snipped fresh parsley
1 teaspoon sugar

In a Dutch oven, brown meat in oil over medium-high heat. Add tomatoes, tomato juice or water, onions, garlic, pepper, and salt if desired. Bring to a boil; reduce heat and simmer for 1 hour. Add potatoes, carrots, corn, green beans, peas and celery. Cover and simmer 30 minutes. Add squash; simmer 10-15 minutes or until meat and vegetables are tender. Stir in parsley and sugar. **Yield:** 16 servings. **Diabetic Exchanges:** One serving (1 cup, without added salt) equals 1 meat, 1 starch, 2 vegetable; also, 189 calories, 170 mg sodium, 32 mg cholesterol, 22 gm carbohydrate, 13 gm protein, 6 gm fat.

CHICKEN AND OKRA GUMBO
Catherine Bouis, Palm Harbor, Florida

(PICTURED ON PAGE 8)

1 broiler-fryer chicken (2-1/2 to 3 pounds), cut up
2 quarts water
1/4 cup cooking oil *or* bacon drippings
2 tablespoons all-purpose flour
2 medium onions, chopped
2 celery stalks, chopped
1 green pepper, chopped
3 garlic cloves, minced
1 can (28 ounces) tomatoes, drained
2 cups sliced fresh *or* frozen okra (1-inch pieces)
2 bay leaves
1 teaspoon dried basil
1 teaspoon salt
1/2 teaspoon pepper
1 to 2 teaspoons hot pepper sauce
2 tablespoons sliced green onions
Chopped fresh parsley
Cooked rice

Place chicken and water in a large kettle. Cover and bring to a boil. Reduce heat to simmer; cook until chicken is tender, about 30-45 minutes. Remove chicken and reserve broth. Bone and cube chicken; set aside. In an 8-qt. kettle, combine oil or drippings and flour until smooth. Cook over medium-high heat for 5 minutes, stirring constantly. Reduce heat to medium. Cook and stir about 5 minutes more or until mixture is reddish-brown (the color of a penny). Turn the heat to high. Stir in 2 cups of reserved broth, mixing well. Cook and stir until thickened. Add onions, celery, green pepper and garlic; cook and stir for 5 minutes. Add tomatoes, okra, bay leaves, basil, salt, pepper and hot pepper sauce. Simmer 1-1/2 to 2 hours; add additional seasonings to taste. Stir in chicken; heat through. Garnish with green onions and parsley. Serve with rice. **Yield:** 8-10 servings.

FREEZER COLESLAW
Patricia Aurand, Arcadia, Ohio

1 medium head cabbage, shredded (about 10 cups)
1 carrot, shredded
1 green pepper, chopped
1 teaspoon salt
1 cup vinegar
2 cups sugar
1 teaspoon celery seed
1 teaspoon mustard seed

In a large bowl, combine vegetables with salt; let stand 1 hour. Place remaining ingredients in a saucepan; bring to a boil and boil for 1 minute. Cool. Drain vegetables and add to vinegar mixture; stir gently. Ladle into plastic freezer containers and freeze. When ready to use, defrost and serve chilled. **Yield:** 1-1/2 to 2 quarts.

BACON-STUFFED BURGERS

Sandy McKenzie, Braham, Minnesota

(PICTURED ON PAGE 8)

4 bacon strips
1/4 cup chopped onion
1 can (4 ounces) mushroom pieces, drained and finely chopped
1 pound lean ground beef
1 pound bulk pork sausage
1/4 cup grated Parmesan cheese
1/2 teaspoon pepper
1/4 teaspoon garlic powder
2 tablespoons steak sauce
8 hamburger buns, split and toasted
Leaf lettuce, optional

Cook bacon until crisp. Remove bacon and discard all but 2 tablespoons drippings. Saute onion in drippings until tender. Crumble bacon; add with mushrooms to skillet and set aside. Meanwhile, combine beef, pork, cheese, pepper, garlic powder and steak sauce in a large bowl. Shape into 16 patties. Divide bacon mixture and place over eight of the patties. Place remaining patties on top and press edges tightly to seal. Grill over medium coals until *well-done* (pork sausage in burgers requires thorough cooking). Serve on buns, with lettuce if desired. **Yield:** 8 servings.

BARLEY BORSCHT

Blanche Babinski, Minto, North Dakota

 This tasty dish uses less sugar, salt and fat. Recipe includes *Diabetic Exchanges.*

2 pounds beef bones
1 medium onion, chopped
1 bay leaf
1 teaspoon salt
10 whole peppercorns
6 cups water
1 medium rutabaga (about 1 pound), diced
3 cups fresh diced beets (about 1-1/2 pounds)
2 cups chopped celery
1 small head cabbage (about 1 pound), shredded
2-1/2 cups diced carrots (about 1 pound)
2-1/2 cups diced peeled potatoes (about 1 pound)
3/4 cup pearl barley
1 can (14-1/2 ounces) tomatoes with liquid, cut up
1/4 cup vinegar
Sour cream, optional
Fresh dill

In a Dutch oven, combine beef bones, onion, bay leaf, salt, peppercorns and water. Bring to a boil; reduce heat. Cover and simmer for 2 hours. Strain broth; discard bones, onion and seasonings. Skim fat and return broth to the kettle. Add rutabaga, beets, celery, cabbage, carrots, potatoes and barley. Return to a boil; reduce heat. Cover and simmer 50 minutes or until vegetables are almost tender and barley is cooked. Stir in tomatoes with liquid and vinegar; heat through. Ladle into serving bowls. Top with a dollop of sour cream if desired. Sprinkle with dill. **Yield:** 16 servings. **Diabetic Exchanges:** One serving (1 cup, without sour cream) equals 1 starch, 1 vegetable; also, 110 calories, 227 mg sodium, 0 mg cholesterol, 26 gm carbohydrate, 3 gm protein, 1 gm fat.

MISSION BAKED BEANS

Mrs. Charles Lewis, Yucaipa, California

(PICTURED ON PAGE 8)

8 bacon strips, cooked and crumbled
1 can (28 ounces) pork and beans
1 can (15-1/2 ounces) chili beans, undrained
3/4 cup finely chopped onion
1/2 cup packed dark brown sugar
1 can (8 ounces) enchilada sauce
1 tablespoon all-purpose flour
2 teaspoons chili powder
1 teaspoon ground cumin
1/8 teaspoon garlic powder
1 cup (4 ounces) shredded Monterey Jack cheese

Combine all ingredients except cheese; mix gently. Place in a greased 2-qt. casserole. Bake, uncovered, at 475° for 15 minutes. Reduce heat to 375°; bake for 30 minutes, stirring occasionally. Sprinkle with cheese; bake 15 minutes longer. **Yield:** 8-10 servings.

BEST BRAN MUFFINS

Suzanne Smith, Framingham, Massachusetts

 This tasty dish uses less sugar, salt and fat. Recipe includes *Diabetic Exchanges.*

1/2 cup rolled oats
1 cup all-purpose flour
1 cup whole wheat flour
1/2 cup all-bran cereal
1/2 teaspoon salt
1 teaspoon baking powder
1 teaspoon baking soda
1 egg, beaten

1/4 cup vegetable oil
1/2 cup molasses
3/4 cup buttermilk
1 can (8 ounces) crushed pineapple in natural juice, undrained
1/2 cup chopped nuts, dates *or* raisins

In a mixing bowl, combine first seven ingredients. Make a well in the center. Combine the egg, oil, molasses, buttermilk and pineapple with juice. Pour into well; mix until dry ingredients are moistened. Stir in nuts, dates or raisins. Fill 18 greased muffin cups 2/3 full. Bake at 400° for 12 minutes or until golden brown. **Yield:** 18 muffins. **Diabetic Exchanges:** One serving (prepared with nuts) equals 1 starch, 1/2 fruit, 1 fat; also, 151 calories, 221 mg sodium, 16 mg cholesterol, 22 gm carbohydrate, 4 gm protein, 6 gm fat.

APPLE HARVEST SQUARES

Maxine Heaney, Providence, Rhode Island

1-1/2 cups all-purpose flour
1/2 teaspoon salt
1 cup sugar, *divided*
1/2 cup butter *or* margarine
4 cups sliced peeled apples
2 tablespoons lemon juice
1 teaspoon ground cinnamon
1 egg, lightly beaten
1/3 cup evaporated milk
1 teaspoon vanilla extract
3/4 cup chopped nuts
1-1/3 cups flaked coconut

In a bowl, combine flour, salt and 1/3 cup sugar. Cut in butter until the mixture resembles fine crumbs; press into the bottom of a greased 13-in. x 9-in. x 2-in. baking pan. Arrange the apple slices on top of crumbs; sprinkle with lemon juice. Combine 1/3 cup sugar with cinnamon; sprinkle over apples. Bake at 375° for 20 minutes. Meanwhile, in a small bowl, combine remaining sugar with the rest of the ingredients. Spoon over baked apples; bake for another 20 minutes or until golden brown. Cut into squares while still warm. **Yield:** about 20 servings.

QUICK 'N' EASY APPETIZERS: Combine ketchup and brown sugar to taste; add cocktail sausages or slices of hot dogs. Heat and serve in a slow cooker or a fondue pot.

• Spread 1 8-oz. package of cream cheese on a large plate. Top with cocktail sauce; sprinkle with drained canned or frozen shrimp. Serve with crackers.

MEALS IN MINUTES

HER JOB in a school cafeteria kept hundreds of hungry youngsters fed... but sometimes had Betty Claycomb of Alverton, Pennsylvania too tired to fix fancy meals for her family.

So, with a husband and two children of her own at home. Betty (who's now retired, but has always loved to cook) turned to Meals in Minutes for help! Here, Betty shares a quick-to-fix standby that she relied on repeatedly.

"Meat loaf was always a family favorite," she relates. "But it took too long to bake. So I devised a stove-top version that didn't require heating up the oven. It's handy even today."

As a matter of fact, it sounds from chatting with her that Betty may need Meals in Minutes more now than ever! "Since retiring, I've been compiling recipes from family and friends into cookbooks," she reports. "I also write a weekly recipe column for a small newspaper in the area."

What does Betty do outside of the kitchen? She loves to take long walks in the country and work in her large garden.

As you can see in the photo above right, Betty's speedy meal includes a rich tomato sauce. So, while the meat loaves are cooking, you'll likely want to boil pasta to accompany them. At the same time, prepare the dilled cucumbers—a light, refreshing side dish.

The meal's topped off with a fruit and cream treat. "I use canned fruit cocktail with fresh bananas in winter," Betty notes. "In summer, we enjoy the fresh berries of the season."

Whatever the season, you'll find her meat loaf meal is a tasty time-saver. Try it in your kitchen soon!

DILLED CUCUMBERS

> 2 medium cucumbers, peeled and thinly sliced
> 1/2 teaspoon salt
> 1/2 cup sour cream
> 1 tablespoon lemon juice
> 2 tablespoons finely chopped green onion
> 1/8 teaspoon pepper
> 1/4 teaspoon sugar
> 1/2 teaspoon dried dill weed

In a small bowl, toss cucumbers with salt. Allow to stand for 10 minutes. Meanwhile, combine all remaining ingredients. Drain cucumbers and combine with sour cream mixture. Chill until ready to serve. **Yield:** 6 servings.

FRUIT AND CREAM DESSERT

> 2 cans (17 ounces *each*) chunky fruit cocktail, drained
> 2 bananas, sliced
> 1 teaspoon lemon juice
> 1/4 cup maraschino cherries
> 1-1/2 cups whipped topping
> 3/4 cup sour cream

In a bowl, combine fruit cocktail, bananas, lemon juice and cherries. In another bowl, combine the whipped topping and sour cream. Refrigerate both bowls until ready to serve. To serve, spoon fruit into individual serving bowls; top with cream mixture. **Yield:** 6 servings.

INDIVIDUAL MEAT LOAVES

> 1 egg, beaten
> 1 cup soft bread cubes
> 1/4 cup milk
> 1-1/2 teaspoons onion salt
> 1 teaspoon dried parsley flakes
> Dash pepper
> 1-1/2 pounds lean ground beef
> 6 sticks (2-1/2 inches x 1/2 inch *each*) cheddar *or* mozzarella cheese

SAUCE:
> 2 cans (15 ounces *each*) tomato sauce
> 1/2 cup chopped onion
> 1 tablespoon dried parsley flakes
> 1/2 teaspoon dried oregano
> 1/4 teaspoon garlic salt

In a mixing bowl, combine first six ingredients. Mix in beef. Divide into six portions. Shape each portion around a cheese stick and form into a loaf. Set aside. In a large skillet, combine all sauce ingredients. Add loaves and spoon sauce over each. Cover and bring to a boil. Reduce heat to simmer; cook until done, about 20 minutes. **Yield:** 6 servings.

13

Make this mouth-watering meat-and-potatoes meal for your family…and don't be surprised if it becomes a regular favorite!

For starters, the California Green Salad—made with chunks of avocado and almonds—will tantalize tastebuds. It's a fitting accompaniment to the juicy, tomato-topped Country Herbed Meat Loaf and creamy Confetti Scalloped Potatoes.

TASTY TRIO! Country Herbed Meat Loaf, Confetti Scalloped Potatoes, California Green Salad (all recipes on page 15).

COUNTRY HERBED MEAT LOAF

Barbara Roy, Middletown, Pennsylvania

(PICTURED ON PAGE 14)

HERB SAUCE:
　1/4 cup olive oil
　8 ounces fresh mushrooms, chopped
　1 large onion, finely chopped
　1 garlic clove, minced
　1 can (28 ounces) tomatoes, crushed
　1 can (6 ounces) tomato paste
　1 teaspoon salt
　1/8 teaspoon pepper
　2 teaspoons sugar
　1 cup water
　1 bay leaf
　2 tablespoons chopped fresh basil *or* 2 teaspoons dried basil
MEAT LOAF:
　2 pounds ground beef *or* combination of ground beef, pork and veal
　1 cup seasoned dry bread crumbs
　3 tablespoons milk
　2 eggs, beaten

In a skillet, heat oil on high. Saute the mushrooms, onion and garlic. Add tomatoes, tomato paste, salt, pepper and sugar. Remove 1-1/2 cups. Add water, bay leaf and basil to skillet. Simmer, uncovered, for 45 minutes, stirring occasionally. Meanwhile, combine all meat loaf ingredients with 1-1/2 cups reserved sauce. Press into a 9-in. x 5-in. x 3-in. loaf pan lined with waxed paper. Unmold onto a roasting pan. Bake at 350° for 45 minutes. Remove from oven; drain. Spread 1/2 cup of herb sauce over top of meat loaf. Return to oven for 15 minutes. Discard bay leaf and serve remaining sauce over individual servings. **Yield:** 8-10 servings.

CONFETTI SCALLOPED POTATOES

Frances Anderson, Boise, Idaho

(PICTURED ON PAGE 14)

1/2 cup butter *or* margarine
1/2 cup chopped onion
　1 package (16 ounces) frozen hash brown potatoes
　1 can (10-3/4 ounces) cream of mushroom soup, undiluted
　1 soup can milk
　1 cup (4 ounces) shredded cheddar cheese
　1 small green pepper, cut into strips

　2 tablespoons chopped pimiento
Dash pepper
　1 cup cheese cracker crumbs, *divided*

In a skillet, melt butter over medium heat. Saute onion until tender. Stir in potatoes, soup and milk. Add cheese, green pepper, pimiento, pepper and 1/2 cup crumbs. Pour into a greased shallow casserole; top with remaining crumbs. Bake at 375° for 35-40 minutes. **Yield:** 6-8 servings.

CALIFORNIA GREEN SALAD

Mrs. William Ellermeyer, Walnut Creek, California

(PICTURED ON PAGE 14)

DRESSING:
　1/2 cup vegetable *or* olive oil
　2 tablespoons vinegar
　2 tablespoons lemon juice
　1/4 to 1/2 teaspoon salt
　1/4 teaspoon dry mustard
　1/4 teaspoon paprika
SALAD:
　1 large head romaine, torn into pieces
　1 avocado, diced
　4 green onions with tops, sliced
　1/4 cup slivered almonds, toasted
　1/4 cup crumbled blue cheese
Dash seasoned salt

In a jar, combine all dressing ingredients; shake well. Cover and refrigerate. Just before serving, toss together romaine, avocado, onions, almonds and blue cheese in a large salad bowl. Sprinkle with seasoned salt. Pour the dressing over salad; toss well to coat. Serve immediately. **Yield:** 6 servings.

PRALINE CHEESECAKE

Jane Owens, Winona, Mississippi

1-1/2 cups graham cracker crumbs
　3 tablespoons sugar
　3 tablespoons butter *or* margarine, melted
　3 packages (8 ounces *each*) cream cheese, softened
3/4 cup packed brown sugar
　2 tablespoons all-purpose flour
　3 eggs
　2 teaspoons vanilla extract
1/2 cup chopped pecans, toasted
Whipped cream
Whole pecans

Combine cracker crumbs, sugar and butter. Press into the bottom of a 9-in. springform pan. Bake at 350° for 10 minutes. Set aside. Meanwhile, beat

cream cheese until smooth in a large mixing bowl. Gradually add brown sugar and flour. Add eggs, one at a time, beating well after each addition. Add vanilla. Stir in chopped pecans. Pour into crust; bake at 350° for 40-45 minutes or until golden brown. Cool 20 minutes. Refrigerate overnight. Just before serving, garnish with whipped cream and pecans. **Yield:** 12-16 servings.

CINNAMON POTATO ROLLS

Mrs. Jonas Schwartz, Berne, Indiana

3/4 cup sugar
3/4 cup hot mashed potatoes
1-1/2 cups warm water (110° to 115°)
　2 packages (1/4 ounce *each*) active dry yeast
1/2 cup butter *or* margarine, softened
　2 eggs
　2 teaspoons salt
6-1/2 cups all-purpose flour
FILLING:
1-1/3 cups packed brown sugar
1/2 teaspoon ground cinnamon
　3 tablespoons cream
　2 tablespoons butter *or* margarine, softened

Confectioners' sugar icing, optional

In a large mixing bowl, combine sugar and mashed potatoes. Add water and yeast; mix well. Cover and let rise in a warm place for 1 hour. Meanwhile, combine filling ingredients and set aside. Stir dough down; mix in butter, eggs and salt. Gradually stir in flour. Turn out onto a lightly floured surface; knead until smooth and elastic, about 6-8 minutes. Divide dough in half. On a floured surface, roll each portion into a 12-in. x 12-in. square. Divide filling and spread over each square to within 1 in. of the edges. Roll up jelly-roll style. Cut each roll into nine slices. Place in a greased 9-in. x 9-in. baking pan. Cover and let rise in a warm place until doubled, about 1 hour. Bake at 350° for 35-40 minutes or until golden. Drizzle with a confectioners' sugar icing if desired. **Yield:** 18 rolls.

BEEF OR CHICKEN ENCHILADAS

Pam Tangbakken, Genesee, Idaho

1 tablespoon butter *or* margarine
2 medium onions, chopped
1 garlic clove, minced
2 tablespoons all-purpose flour
1 cup chicken broth
1 cup milk
2 cans (4 ounces *each*) chopped green chilies
1/4 teaspoon salt
1/4 teaspoon ground cumin
12 flour *or* corn tortillas
1-1/2 cups shredded cooked beef *or* chicken
1 cup (4 ounces) shredded Monterey Jack cheese
1 cup (4 ounces) shredded cheddar cheese
2 green onions with tops, thinly sliced
Sour cream
Salsa

In a saucepan, melt butter over medium heat. Saute onion and garlic until onion is tender. Blend in flour. Stir in broth, milk, chilies, salt and cumin. Cook and stir until thickened and bubbly. Reduce heat; simmer 5 minutes, stirring occasionally. Set aside. Grease a 13-in. x 9-in. x 2-in. baking dish. Spoon a little sauce in the center of each tortilla; spread to edges. Place about 2 tablespoons meat down the center of each tortilla. Combine cheeses; sprinkle 1-2 tablespoons on top of meat. Roll up tortillas and place in baking dish, seam-side down. Pour remaining sauce over. Sprinkle with green onions and remaining cheese. Bake, uncovered, at 350° for 20-30 minutes or until hot and bubbly. Serve with sour cream and salsa. **Yield:** 6 servings.

CHICKEN CHILI

Nancy Robinson, Kansas City, Kansas

2 tablespoons vegetable oil
1 cup chopped onion
1 cup chopped green pepper
2 garlic cloves, minced
4-1/2 cups diced cooked chicken
2 cans (14-1/2 ounces *each*) stewed tomatoes
1 can (15 ounces) pinto beans, drained
2/3 to 3/4 cup mild *or* medium picante sauce
1 teaspoon chili powder
1 teaspoon ground cumin

1/2 teaspoon salt
Optional toppings: shredded cheddar cheese, diced avocado and sour cream

In a Dutch oven, heat oil on medium. Saute onion, green pepper and garlic until tender. Add chicken, tomatoes, beans, picante sauce and seasonings; bring to a boil. Reduce heat; simmer for 20 minutes. Ladle into soup bowls. Top with cheese, avocado and sour cream if desired. **Yield:** 6-8 servings.

HARVARD BEETS

Stella Quade, Carthage, Missouri

3 cups sliced raw beets *or* 2 cans (16 ounces *each*) sliced beets
1/2 cup sugar
1 tablespoon all-purpose flour
1/2 cup white vinegar
1/2 teaspoon salt
2 tablespoons butter *or* margarine

In a saucepan, place raw beets and enough water to cover. Cook until tender, about 15-20 minutes. Drain, reserving 1/4 cup liquid. (If using canned beets, drain and reserve 1/4 cup juice.) In another saucepan, combine sugar, flour, vinegar and reserved beet juice. Cook over low heat until thickened. Stir in beets, salt and butter. Simmer for 10 minutes. **Yield:** 6-8 servings.

PINEAPPLE SHEET CAKE

Kim Miller Spiek, Sarasota, Florida

CAKE:
2 cups all-purpose flour
2 cups sugar
2 eggs
1 cup chopped nuts
2 teaspoons baking soda
1/2 teaspoon salt
1 teaspoon vanilla extract
1 can (20 ounces) crushed pineapple in heavy syrup, undrained
CREAM CHEESE ICING:
1 package (8 ounces) cream cheese, softened
1 box (16 ounces) confectioners' sugar
1/2 cup butter *or* margarine, softened
1 teaspoon vanilla extract
1/2 cup chopped nuts

In a large mixing bowl, combine cake ingredients. Mix until smooth. Pour into a greased 15-in. x 10-in. x 1-in. baking pan. Bake at 350° for 35 minutes. Cool.

Meanwhile, for icing, combine cream cheese, confectioners' sugar, butter and vanilla in a small mixing bowl. Beat until smooth. Spread over cake and sprinkle with nuts. **Yield:** about 24 servings. *Editor's note:* Yes, there is no shortening in this cake.

OVEN-BARBECUED PORK CHOPS

Teresa King, Whittier, California

6 to 8 loin *or* rib pork chops (3/4 inch thick)
1 tablespoon Worcestershire sauce
2 tablespoons vinegar
2 teaspoons brown sugar
1/2 teaspoon pepper
1/2 teaspoon chili powder
1/2 teaspoon paprika
3/4 cup ketchup
1/3 cup hot water

Place chops in a heavy cast-iron skillet. Combine all remaining ingredients; pour over chops. Bake, uncovered, at 375° for 1 hour. **Yield:** 6-8 servings.

ITALIAN CHICKEN

Sherry Adams, Mount Ayr, Iowa

1 broiler/fryer chicken (2-1/2 to 3 pounds), cut up
1/4 cup grated Parmesan cheese
1 jar (30 ounces) spaghetti sauce
1/2 cup sliced fresh mushrooms
1/2 cup sliced black olives
2/3 cup shredded mozzarella cheese
Cooked spaghetti

Place chicken in a 13-in. x 9-in. x 2-in. baking pan. Bake, uncovered, at 350° for 40 minutes. Drain. Sprinkle chicken with Parmesan cheese. Combine spaghetti sauce, mushrooms and olives. (If the sauce is thick, add water.) Pour over chicken; bake for another 20 minutes or until chicken is done. Sprinkle with mozzarella cheese; return to oven just until cheese melts. Serve with spaghetti. **Yield:** 6 servings.

CIDER BAKED SQUASH

Christine Gibson, Fontana, Wisconsin

2 medium acorn squash, sliced into 1-inch circles and seeds removed
1/2 cup apple cider
1/4 cup packed brown sugar

1/2 teaspoon salt
1/8 teaspoon ground cinnamon
1/8 teaspoon ground mace

Place squash in a 15-in. x 10-in. x 1-in. baking pan. Pour cider over squash. Combine all remaining ingredients and sprinkle on top. Cover with foil. Bake at 325° for 45 minutes or until squash is tender. **Yield:** 6 servings.

BLACK BEAN SOUP

Mrs. Albert Lopez, Riverside, California

2 cups dry black beans
2 quarts water
1 medium onion, chopped
1/2 pound lean pork cubes
2 teaspoons salt
3 garlic cloves, minced
1 teaspoon dried oregano
1 can (6 ounces) tomato paste
Optional toppings: thinly sliced
   radishes, finely shredded cabbage,
   minced fresh chili peppers and
   sour cream

Rinse beans. In a Dutch oven, combine beans and water. Bring to a boil. Reduce heat; cover and simmer until beans wrinkle and crack, about 1-1/2 hours. Add onion, pork, salt, garlic and oregano. Simmer, covered, 1-1/2 to 2 hours, or until beans and pork are tender. Stir in tomato paste; heat through. Ladle into soup bowls. If desired, top with radishes, cabbage, peppers and sour cream. **Yield:** 2 quarts.

CABBAGE AND BEEF SOUP

Ethel Ledbetter, Canton, North Carolina

1 pound lean ground beef
1/2 teaspoon garlic salt
1/4 teaspoon garlic powder
1/4 teaspoon pepper
2 celery stalks, chopped
1 can (16 ounces) kidney
   beans, undrained
1/2 medium head cabbage,
   chopped
1 can (28 ounces) tomatoes,
   chopped and liquid reserved
1 tomato can water
4 beef bouillon cubes
Chopped fresh parsley

In a Dutch oven, brown beef. Add all remaining ingredients except parsley; bring to a boil. Reduce heat and simmer, covered, for 1 hour. Garnish with parsley. **Yield:** 3 quarts. *If cooking for two:* Soup can be frozen in serving-size portions to enjoy months later.

GRANDMA'S GELATIN FRUIT SALAD

Wilma McLean, Medford, Oregon

2 cups boiling water, *divided*
1 package (3 ounces)
   lemon-flavored gelatin
2 cups ice cubes, *divided*
1 can (20 ounces) crushed
   pineapple, liquid drained and
   reserved
1 package (3 ounces)
   orange-flavored gelatin
2 cups miniature marshmallows
3 large bananas, sliced
1/2 cup finely shredded cheddar
   cheese
COOKED SALAD DRESSING:
1 cup reserved pineapple juice
1/2 cup sugar
1 egg, beaten
2 tablespoons cornstarch
1 tablespoon butter *or*
   margarine
1 cup whipped topping

In a mixing bowl, combine 1 cup water and lemon gelatin. Add 1 cup ice cubes, stirring until melted. Add pineapple. Pour into a 13-in. x 9-in. x 2-in. baking pan; refrigerate until set. Repeat with orange gelatin, remaining water and ice. Stir in marshmallows. Pour over lemon layer; refrigerate until set. For dressing, combine pineapple juice, sugar, egg, cornstarch and butter in a saucepan. Cook over medium heat, stirring constantly, until thickened. Cover and refrigerate overnight. The next day, arrange bananas over gelatin. Combine dressing with whipped topping; spread over bananas. Sprinkle with cheese. **Yield:** 12-15 servings.

CRUMB CAKE

Rosemary White, Oneida, New York

2 cups packed brown sugar
2-1/2 cups all-purpose flour
1/2 teaspoon salt
1/2 cup butter *or* margarine,
   softened
1 teaspoon ground cinnamon
1/2 cup chopped pecans
1 cup milk
1 tablespoon baking powder
Whipped topping and pecan halves,
optional

In a mixing bowl, combine sugar, flour and salt. Cut in butter until mixture resembles a coarse meal. Remove 1 cup mixture and combine with cinnamon and pecans; set aside. To remaining crumb mixture, add milk and baking powder.

Spread into a greased 13-in. x 9-in. x 2-in. baking pan. Sprinkle the reserved crumb topping over batter. Bake at 350° for 30 minutes or until cake tests done. Cut into squares. Garnish with whipped topping and a pecan half if desired. **Yield:** 12-16 servings.

SCALLOPED CHICKEN

Rosella Bauer, Cissna Park, Illinois

1/2 loaf white bread, cubed
1-1/2 cups cracker crumbs, *divided*
3 cups chicken broth
3 eggs, lightly beaten
1 teaspoon salt
3/4 cup diced celery
2 tablespoons chopped onion
3 cups cubed cooked chicken
1 can (8 ounces) sliced
   mushrooms, drained
1 tablespoon butter *or* margarine

In a mixing bowl, combine bread cubes and 1 cup cracker crumbs. Stir in broth, eggs, salt, celery, onion, chicken and mushrooms. Spoon into a greased 2-qt. casserole. In a saucepan, melt butter; brown remaining cracker crumbs. Sprinkle over casserole. Bake at 350° for 1 hour. **Yield:** 6-8 servings.

POOR MAN'S COOKIES

Georgia Perrine, Bremerton, Washington

2 cups rolled oats
1 cup packed brown sugar
1/2 cup sugar
1 cup all-purpose flour
1/4 teaspoon salt
1 teaspoon baking soda
1/4 cup hot water
1/2 cup shortening, melted and
   cooled
1 teaspoon vanilla extract

In a mixing bowl, combine oats, sugars, flour and salt. In a separate bowl, combine soda and water; stir into oats mixture along with shortening and vanilla. Roll into walnut-size balls. Place on greased cookie sheets. Bake at 350° for 10 minutes or until golden brown. Remove from the oven; allow to stand 2 minutes before removing to a wire rack to cool. **Yield:** about 3-1/2 dozen.

'My Most Memorable Meal'

After marrying a tall Kansas farmer with broad shoulders and a hearty appetite, Hope Huggins of Santa Cruz, California quickly learned that it took an awful lot of cooking to fill him up!

Luckily, Hope learned how to cook long before she got married. By age 7, she was already baking four loaves of bread at a time in her family's old wood-burning range.

"I learned from my mother and grandmother, and making some of those same recipes now takes me back to those times," Hope says. "I can still see Grandmother putting her hand inside that range make sure the temperature was right."

Hope's husband and the rest of her family think he tasty stuffed peppers are just right, too. That's wh Hope selected that family favorite as part of he "Most Memorable Meal". Also included are a tang four-bean salad, orange corn muffins and her favorit dessert, a lemony cheesecake pie.

OLD-FASHIONED FAVORITES. Clockwise from top **Cheesecake Pie, Stuffed Green Peppers, Four-Bean Sa ad, Orange Corn Muffins** (all recipes on page 19).

MEMORABLE MEAL

The first four recipes listed here come from Hope Huggins of Santa Cruz, California (see photo and story at left).

STUFFED GREEN PEPPERS

    5 to 6 medium green peppers
    3/4 cup uncooked brown rice
    1 pound lean ground beef
    1 medium onion, chopped
    1 can (8 ounces) tomato sauce
    1/4 teaspoon dried basil
    1/4 teaspoon dried oregano
    1/4 teaspoon dried thyme
    1/2 teaspoon salt
Pepper to taste
    1/2 teaspoon instant beef
      bouillon granules

Remove tops and seeds from peppers. In a large kettle, bring water to a boil; cook peppers for 5 minutes. Remove and drain. Cook rice according to package directions. In a skillet, brown beef and onion. Drain. Add tomato sauce, herbs, salt and pepper; cook 5 minutes. Stir in rice. Stuff peppers with the beef/rice mixture. Place upright in a shallow baking dish or casserole. Bake at 375° for 15-20 minutes. **Yield:** 5-6 servings. *If cooking for two:* Leftover peppers will freeze well to enjoy later.

ORANGE CORN MUFFINS

    1 cup yellow cornmeal
    1 cup all-purpose flour
    1/3 cup sugar
    4 teaspoons baking powder
    1/4 teaspoon salt
    1 egg, beaten
    1 cup milk
    1/4 cup vegetable oil
    1 tablespoon grated orange peel

In a mixing bowl, combine cornmeal, flour, sugar, baking powder and salt. In another bowl, combine egg, milk, oil and orange peel. Add to cornmeal mixture, stirring just until ingredients are

combined. Fill greased muffin tins 2/3 full. Bake at 425° for 15 minutes or until lightly brown. Remove from the tins and serve warm. **Yield:** 12 muffins. *If cooking for two:* Freeze cooled muffins to enjoy months later.

FOUR-BEAN SALAD

    1 can (16 ounces) green beans,
      drained
    1 can (16 ounces) wax beans,
      drained
    1 can (16 ounces) garbanzo
      beans, rinsed and drained
    1 can (16 ounces) kidney
      beans, rinsed and drained
    1/4 cup slivered green pepper
    8 green onions, sliced
    3/4 cup sugar
    1/2 cup cider vinegar
    1/4 cup vegetable oil
    1/2 teaspoon salt

In a large salad bowl, combine all of the beans, green pepper and onions. In a small bowl, combine remaining ingredients; stir until the sugar dissolves. Pour over bean mixture. Cover and refrigerate overnight, stirring several times. **Yield:** 10-12 servings.

CHEESECAKE PIE

    1-1/4 cups graham cracker crumbs
      (about 18 squares)
    1/3 cup butter *or* margarine, melted
    2 packages (8 ounces *each*)
      cream cheese, softened
    1/2 cup sugar
    2 eggs
    1 teaspoon vanilla extract
    1/2 teaspoon finely grated
      lemon peel
TOPPING:
    1 cup (8 ounces) sour cream
    2 tablespoons sugar
    1/2 teaspoon vanilla extract
Additional lemon peel, optional
Mint leaves, optional

Combine crumbs and butter. Firmly press into the bottom and up the sides of a 9-in. pie plate. Chill. In a small mixing bowl, blend cream cheese, sugar, eggs and vanilla. Stir in lemon peel. Pour into prepared crust; bake at 325° for 25 minutes. Remove from oven. Cool 5 minutes. Meanwhile, in a small bowl, combine sour cream, sugar and vanilla. Spread over pie; bake 5 additional minutes. Cool to room temperature, then refrigerate at least 5 hours. Garnish with additional lemon peel and mint leaves if desired. **Yield:** 6-8 servings.

OLD-FASHIONED RHUBARB CAKE

Marilyn Homola, Hazel, South Dakota

    1/2 cup butter *or* margarine
    1-1/4 cups sugar, *divided*
    1 egg
    1 cup buttermilk
    1 teaspoon vanilla extract
    2 cups all-purpose flour
    1 teaspoon baking soda
    1/2 teaspoon salt
    2 cups chopped rhubarb
    1/2 teaspoon ground cinnamon
MILK TOPPING:
    1-1/2 cups milk
    1/3 cup sugar
    1 teaspoon vanilla extract

In a mixing bowl, cream butter and 1 cup sugar. Add egg; beat well. In a second bowl, combine buttermilk and vanilla; set aside. Combine flour, baking soda and salt; add alternately with buttermilk/vanilla to the creamed mixture. Stir in rhubarb. Spread into a greased 13-in. x 9-in. x 2-in. baking pan. Combine the remaining sugar with cinnamon; sprinkle over batter. Bake at 350° for 35 minutes or until cake tests done. For topping, combine all ingredients; pour over individual squares. **Yield:** 12 servings.

POTATO/SPINACH CASSEROLE

Winifred Winch, Wetmore, Michigan

    6 to 8 large potatoes, peeled,
      cooked and mashed
    1 cup (8 ounces) sour cream
    2 teaspoons salt
    1/4 teaspoon pepper
    2 tablespoons chopped chives
      or green onion tops
    1/4 cup butter *or* margarine
    1 package (10 ounces) frozen
      chopped spinach, thawed and
      well drained
    1 cup (4 ounces) shredded
      cheddar cheese

In a large bowl, combine all ingredients except cheese. Spoon into a greased 2-qt. casserole. Bake, uncovered, at 400° for 15 minutes. Top with cheese and bake 5 minutes longer. **Yield:** 6-8 servings.

PRETTY 'N' SWEET: Add a box of undissolved strawberry gelatin to rhubarb you're using in a recipe, then mix until it is coated or blended in. It adds flavor, sweetens and gives rhubarb a pretty red color.

19

FOR filling and flavorful fare that's quick and easy besides, these speedy recipes just can't be beat!

MINESTRONE IN MINUTES

Sherrie Pfister, Hollandale, Wisconsin

3 links sweet *or* hot Italian sausage, sliced
1 cup chopped onion
1 can (16 ounces) tomatoes with liquid, chopped
2 small zucchini, cubed
3 beef bouillon cubes
3 cups water
2 cups finely chopped cabbage
1 can (16 ounces) great northern beans, undrained
1 teaspoon dried basil
2 tablespoons chopped fresh parsley
Grated Parmesan cheese

In a Dutch oven or soup kettle, brown sausage and onion until onion is tender. Add all remaining ingredients except cheese. Simmer 1 hour. Sprinkle with cheese. **Yield:** 2 quarts.

BLACK BEANS AND SAUSAGE

Sharon Hunt, Spring Hill, Florida

1 tablespoon cooking oil
1 medium onion, chopped
1 can (14-1/2 ounces) stewed tomatoes
1 can (15 ounces) black

SOUP'S ON—THE DOUBLE! Making this minestrone (recipe above) is a quick trick.

beans, undrained
1 teaspoon dried oregano
1/2 teaspoon garlic powder
Salt to taste
1-1/2 cups uncooked instant brown rice
1 pound pork sausage links, cooked and sliced

In a skillet, heat oil. Cook onion until tender. Add the tomatoes, beans and seasonings. Bring to a boil. Stir in rice; reduce heat and simmer 5 minutes. Add sausage and let stand, covered, 5 minutes. **Yield:** 6-8 servings.

BLACK BEAN SALSA

Susan Cochran, Anaheim, California

1 can (15 ounces) black beans, *divided*
2 tablespoons lime juice
2 to 4 tablespoons chopped fresh cilantro
1 medium onion, chopped
1 garlic clove, minced
3 plum tomatoes, seeded and chopped
Salt to taste
Tortilla chips

Drain beans, reserving 1 tablespoon liquid. In a mixing bowl, combine lime juice, half the beans and the reserved bean liquid. Mash until smooth. Stir in remaining beans, cilantro, onion, garlic, tomatoes and salt. Serve with tortilla chips. **Yield:** 4-6 servings.

HOPPING JOHN

Anne Creech, Kinston, North Carolina

1/2 pound bacon, cut into 1-inch pieces
1/2 cup chopped green *or* sweet red pepper
2 celery stalks, chopped
6 green onions, sliced
1 cup uncooked long-grain rice
2 cups water
Salt and pepper to taste
1 teaspoon ground red pepper
1/2 teaspoon dried basil
1/4 teaspoon dried thyme
1/4 teaspoon dried oregano
1 bay leaf
1 can (15 ounces) black-eyed peas, drained

In a skillet, cook bacon until crisp. Remove bacon, reserving 2 tablespoons of the drippings. Saute pepper, celery and

onions until almost tender. Add rice, water and seasonings. Cover and simmer 10 minutes. Add peas and bacon; cook 10 minutes. Remove bay leaf. **Yield:** 4-6 servings.

PINTO BEAN AND RICE CASSEROLE

Linda Emery, Tuckerman, Arkansas

1 can (15 ounces) pinto beans, rinsed and drained
1/2 cup mild *or* hot picante sauce
1 can (15 ounces) Spanish rice
1 pound lean ground beef, cooked and drained
1 cup (4 ounces) shredded cheddar cheese, *divided*
Tortilla chips, optional

In a 1-1/2-qt. casserole, combine the beans, picante sauce, rice, beef and half the cheese. Bake at 350°, uncovered, for about 20-25 minutes or until heated through. Sprinkle with remaining cheese. Serve with tortilla chips if desired. **Yield:** 4-6 servings.

SPEEDY BEAN SOUP

Kathleen Drott, Pineville, Louisiana

2 cans (11-1/2 ounces *each*) condensed bean and bacon soup, undiluted
1 soup can water
3 cans (16 ounces *each*) great northern *or* navy beans, undrained
1 can (15 ounces) jalapeno pinto beans, undrained
1 medium onion, finely chopped
1 teaspoon salt
1/2 teaspoon garlic powder
1/4 teaspoon pepper

In a large Dutch oven or soup kettle, combine all ingredients. Simmer about 20 minutes. **Yield:** 3 quarts.

ODOR-FREE ONION: To rid hands of onion odors, rinse them with fresh undiluted lemon juice. Or rub fingers with celery salt before washing. Or after washing with cold water and salt, rub chlorophyll toothpaste over fingers and rinse well.

ountry cooks have always had a special way of taking basic beans and turning them into "pass the seconds, please!" family favorites—just glance at the imaginative dishes below and on the following two pages for a robust helping of proof. In any season, these taste-tempters are tops at the dinner table.

BEST BEANS! Clockwise from top right: **Maple Baked Beans, Shaker Bean Soup, Spicy Red Beans and Rice, Cathy's Tomato and Bean Salad** (all recipes on page 25).

Beans—a nutritious and delicious staple in country kitchens—are perfect for hearty winter warm-ups as well as simple summer meals. In skillets, bowls and casseroles, these easy bean dishes are delightful, even as leftovers!

RIGHT ON THE *BEAN*. Clockwise from lower left: **Three Bean Casserole** (p. 25), **Carrot/Lentil Salad** (p. 26), **Taco Soup** (p. 26), **Black-Eyed Pea Chowder** (p. 26), **Country Cassoulet** (p. 26), **Chili-Cheese Bake** (p. 26), **White Bean Dip** (p. 26), **Fiesta Appetizer** (p. 27).

reat the family to a hearty new menu by serving the recipes on this page.

Start off the meal with a generous serving of Company Onion Soup garnished with a thick slice of cheese-topped French bread, followed by a crisp Spinach Salad. For the main course, try the North Carolina Shrimp Saute—it's ready in minutes. And for the grand finale pass the luscious Maple Cream Pie ...guaranteed to keep them asking for more!

FOUR-COURSE FEAST. Clockwise from top left: **Spinach Salad** (p. 27), **Maple Cream Pie** (p. 27), **North Carolina Shrimp Saute** (p. 28), **Company Onion Soup** (p. 27).

MAPLE BAKED BEANS

Cindy Huitema, Dunnville, Ontario

(PICTURED ON PAGE 21)

1 pound dry navy beans
4 quarts water, *divided*
6 bacon strips, cut up *or* 1 cup
  cubed cooked ham
1 medium onion, chopped
1 cup maple syrup *or* maple-
  flavored syrup
1/2 cup ketchup
1/4 cup barbecue sauce
5 teaspoons cider vinegar
1 teaspoon prepared mustard
1 teaspoon salt
1/2 teaspoon pepper

Sort and rinse beans; place in a 4-qt. Dutch oven. Cover with 2 qts. cold water. Bring to a boil; reduce heat and simmer for 2 minutes. Remove from the heat. Cover and let stand 1 hour. Drain and rinse beans. Return beans to Dutch oven; cover with remaining water. Bring to a boil; reduce heat and simmer for 30-40 minutes or until almost tender. Drain and reserve liquid. In a 2-1/2-qt. casserole or bean pot, combine beans with all remaining ingredients. Bake, covered, at 300° for 2-1/2 hours or until tender. Stir occasionally; add reserved bean liquid if necessary. **Yield:** 10-12 servings.

SHAKER BEAN SOUP

Deborah Amrine, Grand Haven, Michigan

(PICTURED ON PAGE 21)

1 pound dry great northern beans
Water
1 meaty ham bone *or* 2 smoked
  ham hocks
1 large onion, chopped
3 celery stalks, diced
2 carrots, shredded
Salt to taste
1/2 teaspoon pepper
1/2 teaspoon dried thyme
1 can (28 ounces) crushed
  tomatoes in puree
2 tablespoons brown sugar
1-1/2 cups finely shredded fresh
  spinach leaves

Sort and rinse beans. Place in a Dutch oven or soup kettle; cover with water and bring to a boil. Boil 2 minutes. Remove from the heat; let stand 1 hour. Drain beans and discard liquid. In the same kettle, place ham bone or hocks, 3 qts. water and beans. Bring to a boil; reduce heat and simmer, covered, 1-1/2 hours or until meat easily falls from the bone. Remove bones from broth

and, when cool enough to handle, trim meat. Discard bones. Add ham, onion, celery, carrots, salt, pepper and thyme. Simmer, covered, 1 hour or until beans are tender. Add tomatoes and brown sugar. Cook for 10 minutes. Just before serving, add spinach. **Yield:** 5 quarts.

SPICY RED BEANS
AND RICE

Rebecca Michael, San Diego, California

(PICTURED ON PAGE 21)

1 pound dry red kidney beans
2 teaspoons paprika
1/2 to 1 teaspoon cayenne pepper
1 teaspoon freshly ground
  black pepper
2 bay leaves
1 teaspoon ground cumin
1 quart water
1 large smoked ham hock
2 to 3 teaspoons salt
1-1/2 cups chopped celery
1-1/2 cups chopped onion
2 garlic cloves, minced
1/2 teaspoon hot pepper sauce
3 tablespoons minced fresh
  parsley
Cooked rice

Sort and rinse beans. In a large Dutch oven or kettle, place all ingredients except parsley and rice. Bring to a boil, then simmer, covered, 3 to 4 hours or until beans are tender. Stir occasionally, adding water as needed to make a thick gravy. Just before serving, remove bay leaves and stir in parsley. Serve over rice. **Yield:** 8 servings.

CATHY'S TOMATO AND
BEAN SALAD

Cathy Meizel, Flanders, New York

(PICTURED ON PAGE 21)

 This tasty dish uses less sugar, salt and fat. Recipe includes *Diabetic Exchanges*.

1 can (15 ounces) garbanzo
  beans, rinsed and drained
4 large ripe tomatoes, sliced
  thick

1 cup thinly sliced red onion
1 can (6 ounces) medium pitted
  ripe olives, drained and halved
1/2 cup olive oil
5 to 6 large fresh basil leaves,
  snipped *or* 1 tablespoon
  dried basil
1/2 teaspoon dried oregano
1/4 teaspoon pepper
Salt to taste
1/8 teaspoon garlic powder

In a large salad bowl, layer beans, tomatoes, onion and olives. Combine all remaining ingredients; pour over vegetables. Cover and chill at least 3 hours or overnight. Serve chilled or at room temperature. **Yield:** 8 servings. **Diabetic Exchanges:** One serving (without added salt) equals 1 starch, 1 vegetable, 2 fat; also, 178 calories, 333 mg sodium, 0 mg cholesterol, 19 gm carbohydrate, 4 gm protein, 10 gm fat.

THREE BEAN CASSEROLE

Georgia Hennings, Alliance, Nebraska

(PICTURED ON PAGE 22)

1 can (15 to 16 ounces) red
  kidney beans, rinsed and
  drained
1 can (15 ounces) garbanzo
  beans, rinsed and drained
1 can (16 ounces) lima beans,
  rinsed and drained
1 pound lean ground beef
1 large onion, chopped
1 garlic clove, minced
1/4 cup packed brown sugar
1/2 teaspoon salt
Dash pepper
2 tablespoons prepared mustard
1/2 cup ketchup
1 teaspoon ground cumin
1/4 cup water
1 tablespoon vinegar

In a 2-1/2-qt. casserole, combine beans; set aside. In a skillet, cook beef, onion and garlic until beef is no longer pink. Remove from the heat; drain. Add remaining ingredients to skillet; mix well. Stir beef mixture into beans. Bake at 350° for 45 minutes or until heated through. **Yield:** 6-8 servings.

CARROT/LENTIL SALAD

Monica Wilcott, Sturgis, Saskatchewan

(PICTURED ON PAGE 22)

✓ This tasty dish uses less sugar, salt and fat. Recipe includes *Diabetic Exchanges*.

1 cup dry lentils
1 cup diced carrots
2 garlic cloves, minced
1 bay leaf
DRESSING:
1/2 cup finely chopped celery
1/4 cup finely chopped fresh parsley
1/4 cup olive oil
1/4 cup lemon juice
1 teaspoon salt
1/2 teaspoon dried thyme
1/4 teaspoon pepper

In a Dutch oven, combine lentils, carrots, garlic and bay leaf. Cover with 1 in. of water. Bring to a boil, then simmer 15-20 minutes or until lentils are tender. Remove bay leaf; drain and cool. Meanwhile, combine all ingredients for dressing. Pour over lentil mixture. Cover and refrigerate several hours. **Yield:** 6 servings. **Diabetic Exchanges:** One serving equals 1-1/2 vegetable, 1 starch, 2 fat; also, 202 calories, 403 mg sodium, 0 mg cholesterol, 23 gm carbohydrate, 8 gm protein, 9 gm fat.

TACO SOUP

Tonya Jones, Sundown, Texas

(PICTURED ON PAGE 22)

2 pounds lean ground beef
1 small onion, chopped
3 cans (4 ounces *each*) chopped green chilies
1 teaspoon salt
1 teaspoon pepper
1 can (15 to 16 ounces) pinto beans, rinsed and drained
1 can (16 ounces) lima beans, rinsed and drained
1 package (1-1/4 ounces) taco seasoning
1-1/2 cups water
1 package (1 ounce) ranch dressing mix
1 can (14-1/2 ounces) hominy, drained
3 cans (14-1/2 ounces *each*) stewed tomatoes
1 can (15 to 16 ounces) red kidney beans, rinsed and drained
Shredded cheddar cheese, optional
Tortilla chips, optional

In a large Dutch oven or kettle, brown beef and onion. Drain. Add all remaining ingredients except last two; bring to a boil. Reduce heat and simmer 30 minutes. Top with cheese and serve with chips if desired. **Yield:** 10 servings.

CHILI-CHEESE BAKE

Rosemary West, Topsham, Maine

(PICTURED ON PAGE 23)

3 cups cooked rice
2 garlic cloves, minced
1 can (4 ounces) chopped green chilies
2 teaspoons chili powder
1/2 teaspoon salt
1 can (15 to 16 ounces) red kidney beans, rinsed and drained
1 medium onion, chopped
2 teaspoons ground cumin
1 teaspoon dried oregano
1 teaspoon creole seasoning
2 cups (8 ounces) shredded cheddar cheese, *divided*

In a greased 2-qt. saucepan, combine all ingredients except cheese. Top with 1-1/2 cups of cheese. Bake, covered, at 350° for 25 minutes. Top with remaining cheese, then bake, uncovered, 10 minutes more. **Yield:** 6 servings.

COUNTRY CASSOULET

Roberta Strohmaier, Lebanon, New Jersey

(PICTURED ON PAGE 23)

3 cups water
3/4 pound dry navy beans
1 bay leaf
1 teaspoon salt
1/4 teaspoon pepper
1 can (14-1/2 ounces) chicken broth
1/4 pound bacon, diced
4 chicken legs *or* thighs
2 carrots, quartered
2 medium onions, quartered
1/4 cup coarsely chopped celery with leaves
1 can (8 ounces) tomatoes, chopped, liquid reserved
2 garlic cloves, crushed
1/2 teaspoon dried marjoram leaves
1/2 teaspoon ground sage
1 teaspoon whole cloves
1/2 pound smoked sausage, cut into 2-inch pieces
Chopped fresh parsley

In a large skillet, combine water, beans, bay leaf, salt and pepper. Bring to a boil;

boil, uncovered, for 2 minutes. Remove from the heat. Cover and let soak for 1 hour. Add chicken broth; cover and cook 1 hour. Meanwhile, fry bacon until crisp. Remove bacon and reserve 2 tablespoons of the drippings. Brown chicken; set aside. In a 3-qt. casserole, mix beans and cooking liquid, bacon, carrots, onions, celery, tomatoes, garlic, marjoram and sage. Sprinkle with cloves; top with chicken. Cover and bake at 350° for 1 hour. Add sausage. Uncover; bake about 30 minutes more or until beans are tender. Discard bay leaf. Garnish with chopped parsley. Recipe may be doubled. **Yield:** 4 servings.

BLACK-EYED PEA CHOWDER

Brenda Bates, Mesquite, Texas

(PICTURED ON PAGE 22)

1 pound bacon
1 cup chopped celery
1 cup chopped onion
1 cup chopped green pepper
2 cans (16 ounces *each*) black-eyed peas, rinsed and drained
1 can (10-1/2 ounces) beef consomme
2 cans (14-1/2 ounces *each*) stewed tomatoes

In a saucepan, cook bacon until crisp. Remove bacon; crumble and set aside. Discard all but 2 tablespoons of drippings; saute celery, onion and green pepper until tender. Add bacon and all remaining ingredients; heat through. **Yield:** 2-1/4 quarts.

WHITE BEAN DIP

Linn Landry, Honeydew, California

(PICTURED ON PAGE 23)

✓ This tasty dish uses less sugar, salt and fat. Recipe includes *Diabetic Exchanges*.

1 can (15 to 16 ounces) cannellini beans *or* great northern beans, rinsed and drained
1 tablespoon lemon juice
2 tablespoons plain yogurt
2 tablespoons chopped fresh parsley
1/2 teaspoon freshly ground black pepper
1/4 teaspoon hot pepper sauce
2 to 3 garlic cloves
Salt to taste
Pita bread, corn chips *or* vegetable dippers

In a food processor or blender, combine all ingredients except for last one. Cover and process until smooth. Chill. Serve with toasted pita bread triangles, corn chips or fresh vegetables. **Yield: 1-1/4 cups. Diabetic Exchanges:** One tablespooon serving (prepared with skim yogurt and no added salt) equals 1/2 starch; also, 29 calories, 78 mg sodium, trace cholesterol, 6 gm carbohydrate, 2 gm protein, trace fat.

FIESTA APPETIZER

Clarice Schweitzer, Sun City, Arizona

(PICTURED ON PAGE 22)

- 1 can (16 ounces) refried beans
- 1 package (1-1/4 ounces) taco seasoning
- 3 ripe avocados
- 1 tablespoon lemon juice
- 1/4 cup sour cream
- 1 can (2-1/4 ounces) sliced ripe olives, drained
- 1 can (4 ounces) chopped green chilies, drained
- 2 medium tomatoes, chopped
- 6 green onions, sliced
- 1 cup (4 ounces) shredded cheddar cheese

Tortilla chips

Combine beans and taco seasoning. Spread mixture on a round 12-in. serving platter. Mash avocados with lemon juice. Spread over beans. Spread sour cream over avocado. Sprinkle olives, chilies, tomatoes, onions and cheese over sour cream. Serve with tortilla chips. **Yield: 8-10 servings.**

MAPLE CREAM PIE

Emma Magielda, Amsterdam, New York

(PICTURED ON PAGE 24)

PASTRY:
- 1 cup all-purpose flour
- 1/4 teaspoon salt
- 3 tablespoons butter *or* margarine
- 3 tablespoons lard
- 2 to 3 tablespoons milk

FILLING:
- 1-3/4 cups milk, *divided*
- 1/4 cup cornstarch
- 3/4 cup plus 1 tablespoon maple *or* maple-flavored syrup, *divided*
- 1/4 teaspoon salt
- 2 egg yolks
- 2 tablespoons butter *or* margarine
- 1 cup whipping cream

Sliced almonds, toasted

Combine the flour and salt in a mixing bowl. Cut in butter and lard until mixture resembles a coarse meal. Sprinkle in milk, 1 tablespoon at a time, mixing until flour is moistened. Shape into a ball. Roll out on a lightly floured surface. Place in a 9-in. pie plate. Trim and flute edges. Prick the bottom and sides with a fork. Bake at 450° for 12-15 minutes or until lightly browned. Cool. For filling, blend together 1/4 cup milk and cornstarch in a saucepan. Gradually stir in remaining milk, 3/4 cup of the syrup and salt. Cook over medium heat, stirring constantly, until mixture comes to a boil. Remove from the heat. Stir about 1/4 cup of the hot mixture into the yolks; return all to the saucepan. Cook, stirring constantly, until thickened and bubbly. Remove from the heat; stir in butter. Cool thoroughly, stirring frequently. Meanwhile, whip cream until stiff. Fold 1 cup into cooled filling; spoon into prepared pie crust. Fold remaining syrup into remaining cream; frost top of pie. Chill for several hours. Garnish with toasted almonds. **Yield: 8 servings.**

COMPANY ONION SOUP

Rose Marie Moore, Walla Walla, Washington

(PICTURED ON PAGE 24)

- 4 tablespoons unsalted butter
- 4 large sweet *or* Walla Walla onions, sliced
- 1 tablespoon sugar
- 6 cups beef broth, *divided*
- 2 tablespoons Worcestershire sauce

Salt and pepper to taste
- 4 thick slices French bread

Additional unsalted butter
Garlic salt *or* 1 garlic clove, halved
- 1 cup (4 ounces) shredded Gruyere *or* Swiss cheese

In a Dutch oven, melt butter over medium heat. Saute onions until tender. Sprinkle sugar over onions. Reduce heat and cook, stirring occasionally, until onions are caramelized, about 20 minutes. Add 3 cups broth; simmer 15 minutes. Add remaining broth, Worcestershire sauce, salt and pepper. Cover and simmer for 30-40 minutes. Meanwhile, spread both sides of the bread with additional butter; sprinkle with garlic salt or rub with the cut-side of garlic clove. Broil bread until golden brown, then turn and brown other side. Ladle soup into individual ovenproof soup bowls. Float a slice of bread in each bowl and sprinkle with cheese. Broil until cheese is melted and bubbly. Serve immediately. **Yield: 4 servings.**

MEXICAN LASAGNA

Ellene Whitworth, Weatherford, Texas

- 1 pound lean ground beef, raw
- 1 can (16 ounces) refried beans
- 2 teaspoons dried oregano
- 1 teaspoon ground cumin
- 3/4 teaspoon garlic powder
- 12 uncooked lasagna noodles
- 2-1/2 cups water
- 2-1/2 cups picante sauce *or* salsa
- 2 cups (16 ounces) sour cream
- 3/4 cup finely sliced green onions
- 1 can (2.2 ounces) sliced black olives, drained
- 1 cup (4 ounces) shredded Monterey Jack cheese

Combine raw beef, beans, oregano, cumin and garlic powder. Place four of the uncooked lasagna noodles in the bottom of a 13-in. x 9-in. x 2-in. baking pan. Spread half the beef mixture over the noodles. Top with four more noodles and the remaining beef mixture. Cover with remaining noodles. Combine water and picante sauce. Pour over all. Cover tightly with foil; bake at 350° for 1-1/2 hours or until noodles are tender. Combine sour cream, onions and olives. Spoon over casserole; top with cheese. Bake, uncovered, until cheese is melted, about 5 minutes. **Yield: 12 servings.**

SPINACH SALAD

Irene Leopold, Colby, Kansas

(PICTURED ON PAGE 24)

DRESSING:
- 1/2 cup packed brown sugar
- 1/2 cup salad oil
- 1/3 cup vinegar
- 1/3 cup ketchup
- 1 tablespoon Worcestershire sauce

SALAD:
- 2 quarts fresh spinach leaves, torn
- 1 can (16 ounces) bean sprouts, drained *or* 2 cups fresh bean sprouts
- 1 can (8 ounces) sliced water chestnuts, drained
- 4 hard-cooked eggs, peeled and diced
- 6 bacon strips, cooked and crumbled
- 1 small onion, thinly sliced

In a bottle or jar, combine all dressing ingredients. Shake well to mix. Set aside. In a large salad bowl, toss all salad ingredients. Just before serving, pour dressing over salad and toss. **Yield: 8 servings.**

NORTH CAROLINA SHRIMP SAUTE

Teresa Hildreth, Stoneville, North Carolina

(PICTURED ON PAGE 24)

1/4 cup butter *or* margarine
1 pound raw shrimp, peeled and deveined
1/2 pound fresh mushrooms, sliced
1 small green pepper, chopped
3 garlic cloves, minced
8 ounces linguini *or* spaghetti
1/2 cup grated Romano cheese
1/2 teaspoon salt
1/4 teaspoon pepper
Chopped fresh parsley
Lemon slices

In a skillet, melt butter over medium heat. Add shrimp, mushrooms, green pepper and garlic. Saute until shrimp turn pink, about 3-5 minutes. Meanwhile, cook pasta according to package directions; drain and place on a large serving platter. Top with shrimp mixture. Sprinkle with cheese, salt, pepper and parsley. Toss well; garnish with lemon. Serve immediately. **Yield:** 4 servings.

HOT KIPPERED SALMON

Barbara Njaa, Nikiski, Alaska

2 salmon fillets (about 2 pounds *each*)
4 teaspoons salt
Pepper to taste
2 tablespoons plus 2 teaspoons brown sugar
2 tablespoons liquid smoke

Place fillets skin side down, side by side, in a greased shallow baking pan. Sprinkle with salt, pepper and brown sugar; drizzle with liquid smoke. Cover and refrigerate 4-8 hours. Drain any liquid. Bake at 350° for 30-45 minutes or until fish flakes with a fork. **Yield:** 8 servings.

CORNMEAL SCRAPPLE

Mrs. Merlin Brubaker, Bettendorf, Iowa

1 cup white *or* yellow cornmeal
1 cup milk
1 teaspoon sugar
1 teaspoon salt
2-3/4 cups boiling water
8 ounces bulk pork sausage, cooked, drained and crumbled
All-purpose flour
2 tablespoons butter *or* margarine

Maple syrup, optional

In a saucepan, combine the cornmeal, milk, sugar and salt; gradually stir in water. Cook and stir until thickened and bubbly. Reduce heat; cook, covered, 10 minutes longer or until very thick, stirring occasionally. Remove from the heat and stir in sausage. Pour into a greased 7-1/2-in. x 3-1/2-in. x 2-in. loaf pan (the pan will be very full). Cover with plastic wrap and refrigerate. To serve, unmold and cut into 1/3-in. slices. Dip both sides in flour. In a skillet, melt butter over medium heat; brown scrapple on both sides. Serve with maple syrup if desired. **Yield:** 6 servings.

SOUTHWESTERN SPOON BREAD

Aldine Fouse, Farmington, New Mexico

1 can (16-1/2 ounces) cream-style corn
1 cup yellow cornmeal
3/4 cup milk
1/3 cup vegetable oil
2 eggs, lightly beaten
1 teaspoon baking powder
1/2 teaspoon salt
1 can (4 ounces) chopped green chilies, drained
1 cup (4 ounces) shredded cheddar cheese

In a mixing bowl, stir together all ingredients except last two. Pour half the batter into a greased 2-qt. baking dish. Sprinkle with chilies and cheese. Pour remaining batter over all. Bake at 375° for 45 minutes or just until set. Serve warm with a spoon. **Yield:** about 6-8 servings.

NORWEGIAN COLESLAW

Gerry Beveridge, Beaufort, North Carolina

1 medium head cabbage
1 tablespoon salt
1-1/2 cups sugar
1 cup vinegar
1 teaspoon mustard seed
1 teaspoon celery seed
2 cups chopped celery
1 small green pepper, chopped
1 small sweet red pepper, chopped
2 carrots, shredded

Shred cabbage and toss with salt. Cover and refrigerate at least 2 hours. In a saucepan, heat sugar, vinegar, mustard and celery seeds. Cook until the sugar dissolves, about 10 minutes. Cool completely. Add to the cabbage along with remaining vegetables; toss.

Cover and refrigerate at least 1 week before serving. Keeps for 4-6 weeks in the refrigerator. **Yield:** 12-16 servings.

OATMEAL VALENTINE COOKIES

Louise Carter, Shepherdstown, West Virginia

2-1/2 cups all-purpose flour
1 teaspoon baking powder
1/2 teaspoon salt
3/4 cup butter *or* margarine, room temperature
3/4 cup sugar
2 tablespoons milk
1 egg
1 teaspoon vanilla extract
1 cup rolled oats
Decorative red sugar, optional

Sift together flour, baking powder and salt. Place in a large mixing bowl along with butter, sugar, milk, egg and vanilla; beat until smooth. Stir in oats. On a floured board, roll the dough to 1/8-in. thickness. Cut into heart shapes; decorate with red sugar if desired. Bake on an ungreased cookie sheet at 375° for 15-18 minutes or until light golden brown. Remove from cookie sheet and cool on wire racks. **Yield:** 2-1/2 dozen 3-inch cookies.

PASTA/SAUSAGE SOUP

Alice Rabe, Beemer, Nebraska

1-1/2 pounds hot *or* sweet Italian sausage
1 medium onion, chopped
1 medium green pepper, cut into strips
1 garlic clove, minced
1 can (28 ounces) tomatoes, chopped, liquid reserved
2 to 2-1/2 cups uncooked bow tie pasta
6 cups water
1 tablespoon sugar
1 tablespoon Worcestershire sauce
2 chicken bouillon cubes
1 teaspoon dried basil
1 teaspoon dried thyme
1 teaspoon salt

Remove casings from the sausages and cut into 1-in. pieces. In a Dutch oven, brown sausage over medium heat. Remove sausage and drain all but 2 tablespoons of the drippings. Saute onion, pepper and garlic until tender. Add sausage and all remaining ingredients. Simmer, uncovered, stirring occasionally, until pasta is tender, about 15-20 minutes. **Yield:** 3 quarts.

MEALS IN MINUTES

YEARS AGO, as a newlywed, Alpha Wilson of Roswell, New Mexico was already adept at making minutes count in the kitchen.

"I was raised on a farm," she explains. "When the chores ran late, my mom and I had to come up with quick and hearty meals. Later, I often used those recipes for my own family."

Nowadays, she's retired. But Alpha still relies on Meals in Minutes menus to make time for her favorite activities. When she's not walking her two dogs or tending to her many plants, she's an avid quilter—last year, she painstakingly restored *seven* heirlooms.

Alpha and her husband, Thomas, also like to pack their camper and head for parts unknown. On the road as well as at home, they'll often enjoy the Barbecue Beef Sandwiches that she shares below. Alpha likes serving the sandwiches with her crunchy stuffed celery and pretty pepper salad. For dessert, her peach crisp's always in season.

Try this tasty combination in your kitchen (or camper!) soon.

BARBECUE BEEF SANDWICHES

- 1 tablespoon butter *or* margarine
- 1 pound lean ground beef
- 1/2 cup chopped onion
- 1 medium green pepper, chopped
- 3/4 cup ketchup
- 1/4 cup water
- 1 tablespoon sugar
- 2 tablespoons prepared mustard
- 1 tablespoon vinegar

Salt and pepper to taste
Hamburger buns

In a skillet, melt butter over medium-high heat. Brown the beef, onion and green pepper. Add all remaining ingredients except buns. Simmer, uncovered, 15 minutes. Serve on buns. **Yield:** about 6 servings.

STUFFED CELERY STALKS

- 1 package (3 ounces) cream cheese, softened
- 2 tablespoons creamy peanut butter
- 1 tablespoon light cream
- 1-1/2 teaspoons minced onion
- 1/4 teaspoon curry powder
- 4 celery stalks, cut into 3-inch pieces
- 1/4 cup chopped salted peanuts

In a small bowl, blend first five ingredients. Stuff into celery pieces; sprinkle with peanuts. Chill until serving. **Yield:** 6-8 servings.

PEPPER SALAD

- 1 green pepper, thinly sliced
- 1 sweet red pepper, thinly sliced
- 1 pound fresh mushrooms, sliced

- 3 tablespoons vinegar
- 1/4 cup vegetable oil
- 1/2 teaspoon salt
Dash pepper
Dash garlic powder, optional

In a bowl, toss peppers and mushrooms. Combine all remaining ingredients and toss with vegetables. Cover and refrigerate until serving. **Yield:** 6-8 servings.

SPICY PEACH CRISP

- 1 can (29 ounces) sliced peaches, well drained
- 1/2 cup rolled oats
- 1/2 cup packed brown sugar
- 1/4 cup all-purpose flour
- 1/4 teaspoon ground cinnamon
- 1/4 teaspoon ground nutmeg
- 1/4 teaspoon ground allspice
- 1/4 cup butter *or* margarine
Cream *or* ice cream

Arrange peaches in an 8-in. x 8-in. pan. In a small bowl, combine oats, sugar, flour and spices. Cut in butter until coarse crumbs form; sprinkle over peaches. Bake at 400° for 15-20 minutes. Serve warm with cream or ice cream. **Yield:** 6-8 servings.

NEED a sweet-tart treat in a hurry? Take your pick from these delicious cherry-quick recipes!

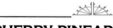

CHERRY ANGEL DELIGHT

Ida Wing, Cape Cod, Massachusetts

1 large prepared angel food cake
1 can (21 ounces) cherry pie filling
1 package (3.4 ounces) instant vanilla pudding mix
1-1/2 cups cold milk
1 cup (8 ounces) sour cream

Cut or tear cake into 1/2-in. pieces to measure 8 cups. Place half the cake cubes in a 9-in. x 9-in. baking pan. Reserve 1/3 cup of pie filling; spread remaining filling over cake. Top with remaining cake cubes. Combine the pudding mix, milk and sour cream. Spoon over cake. Cover and chill. To serve, cut into squares and top with reserved cherries. **Yield:** 9 servings.

CHERRY PINEAPPLE CAKE

Elaine De Rue, Hilton, New York

2 cans (16 ounces *each*) pitted tart red cherries, drained
1 can (20 ounces) crushed pineapple in syrup, undrained
1/3 cup finely chopped walnuts
1 package (18-1/4 ounces) white cake mix (without pudding)
1/2 cup butter *or* margarine, melted
Whipped cream, optional

HASTE MAKES...CAKES! Tempting angel food treats (recipe above) fly from start to finish.

Spread cherries and pineapple with syrup over the bottom of an ungreased 13-in. x 9-in. x 2-in. baking pan. Top with nuts. Sprinkle dry cake mix over all. Pour butter evenly over cake mix. Bake at 350° for 1 hour. Cool. Invert onto a serving plate. Cut into squares. Top with whipped cream if desired. **Yield:** 12-15 servings.

BING CHERRY SALAD

Cindy Mahn, Huntley, Montana

1 can (16 ounces) pitted dark sweet cherries, juice reserved
1 package (8 ounces) cream cheese, softened
1 cup drained crushed pineapple
1 carton (8 ounces) frozen whipped topping, thawed
2 cups miniature marshmallows

Drain cherries and reserve 1/4 cup juice. In a mixing bowl, whip juice with cream cheese. Stir in cherries, pineapple, topping and marshmallows. Chill until ready to serve. **Yield:** 6-8 servings.

CHERRY SQUARES

Mildred Schwartzentruber, Tavistock, Ontario

1-3/4 cups flaked coconut
1/2 cup butter *or* margarine, softened
1/2 cup sugar
1-1/2 cups all-purpose flour
1 can (21 ounces) cherry pie filling

In a mixing bowl, combine first four ingredients. Press half the mixture into the bottom of a greased 9-in. x 9-in. baking pan. Top with the pie filling and sprinkle with remaining crumb mixture. Bake at 375° for 40 minutes or until golden brown. **Yield:** 9 servings.

CHERRY ICE CREAM

Carol Dale, Greenville, Texas

6 eggs
1-1/2 cups sugar
1-1/2 cups milk
1 can (21 ounces) cherry pie filling
1 quart cream
1 can (14 ounces) sweetened

condensed milk
1 tablespoon vanilla extract
1 teaspoon almond extract

In a mixing bowl, beat the eggs and sugar until thick and lemon-colored. Scald milk; slowly pour into egg mixture, stirring constantly, until sugar is dissolved. Cool. Chop the cherries by hand or in a food processor. Combine cherries with egg mixture and all remaining ingredients. Freeze in an ice cream maker. **Yield:** about 1 gallon.

INDIVIDUAL CHERRY CHEESECAKES

Marian Platt, Sequim, Washington

24 vanilla wafer cookies
2 packages (8 ounces *each*) cream cheese, softened
3/4 cup sugar
2 eggs
1 teaspoon vanilla extract
1 can (21 ounces) cherry pie filling
Whipped topping

Place one cookie each in the bottom of 24 greased muffin cups. In a mixing bowl, beat cream cheese and sugar until smooth. Add eggs and vanilla; beat well. Divide filling into each muffin cup. Bake at 375° for 20 minutes. Chill before removing from cups. To serve, top each cheesecake with pie filling and a spoonful of whipped topping. **Yield:** 24 servings.

CHERRY SAUCE

Kathy Emberton, Cicero, Indiana

1 can (16 ounces) pitted tart red cherries, juice reserved
1/4 cup sugar
2 tablespoons cornstarch
1 tablespoon butter *or* margarine
1/4 teaspoon vanilla extract
Few drops red food coloring, optional
Sponge cake, pound cake *or* ice cream

Drain cherries and set aside. Add enough water to juice to equal 1-1/4 cups. In a saucepan, combine sugar and cornstarch. Stir in juice. Cook, stirring constantly, until thick. Remove from the heat. Stir in butter, vanilla, cherries and food coloring if desired. Serve warm over cake or ice cream. **Yield:** 4-6 servings.

Four cheers—and more—for cherries! There's a scrumptious—and sometimes surprising—variety of great country eating that includes that delectable red fruit. Below and on the next two pages, you'll find appetizing new ideas for breakfast treats...mmm-good glaze for ham...spicy salsa and even a soup.

CHERRY BEST. Clockwise from top right: **Cherry Crisp, Cherry Cheesecake Tarts, Cherry/Rhubarb Cobbler, Cherry Cream Scones** (all recipes on page 36).

I t's a cherry jubilee! From spicy salsa to down-home deep-dish pie, cherries add a delicious touch of color to country tables. The dishes shown here will brighten up meals from breakfast to dinner—and right on through dessert.

BRIGHT IDEAS. Clockwise from lower left: **Northwest Cherry Salsa** (p. 36), **Creamy Cherry Cheesecake** (p. 36), **Cherry/Almond Ham Glaze** (p. 37), **Easy Cherry Fruit Soup** (p. 37), **Cherry Cinnamon Dessert Ring** (p. 37), **Cherry/Nut Breakfast Rolls** (p. 37), **Cherry Chewbilees** (p. 37), **Deep-Dish Cherry Pie** (p. 38).

MEN WHO RUN THE RANGE

Featuring favorite recipes from men who love to cook.

MONTANA MOUNTAIN MUFFINS

David Wallace-Menard, Shepherd, Montana

4 cups all-purpose flour
4 cups whole bran cereal
1-1/2 cups sugar
1 tablespoon baking soda
4 teaspoons baking powder
2 teaspoons salt
2 cups cold coffee
2 cups milk
6 eggs, beaten
1-1/2 cups vegetable oil
2 teaspoons vanilla extract
2 cups raisins

In a large mixing bowl, stir together the first six ingredients. Combine remaining ingredients. Stir into the mixing bowl; mix only until dry ingredients are moistened. Cover and refrigerate until ready to bake. Batter will keep for several weeks. When ready to bake, stir batter and fill greased muffin tins 2/3 full. Bake at 350° for 20 minutes or until muffins test done. **Yield:** about 5 dozen.

GARDEN PASTA SALAD

Bernie Bellin, Franklin, Wisconsin

8 ounces corkscrew *or* cartwheel pasta
3 cups assorted chopped fresh *or* frozen vegetables
1 bottle (16 ounces) zesty Italian salad dressing, *divided*
1 cup cubed cooked chicken, turkey *or* ham
1 cup cubed cheddar, mozzarella *or* Monterey Jack cheese
1 can (2-1/2 ounces) sliced ripe olives, drained

Minced fresh parsley *or* basil, optional

Cook pasta according to package directions. Drain but do not rinse. Put pasta back into the kettle. While pasta is hot, toss with the vegetables. Cover for 3-5 minutes. Vegetables will lightly steam in pasta. Place pasta in a large salad bowl. Top with 3/4 of the dressing and lightly toss. Chill several hours or overnight. If pasta is dry, add remaining dressing along with meat, cheese, olives, and parsley or basil if desired. Chill until ready to serve. **Yield:** 6-8 servings.

CHERRY RICE FLUFF

Frank Newton, St. Thomas, Ontario

1-1/2 cups cooked rice
1 teaspoon butter *or* margarine, softened
1/4 teaspoon salt
1 cup milk, *divided*
1 package (3 ounces) cherry-flavored gelatin
1-1/2 cups water
1/4 teaspoon almond extract
1/2 cup whipping cream
2 tablespoons sugar
1 can (16 ounces) pitted red cherries, halved and drained with juice reserved

GLAZE:
Reserved cherry juice
1 tablespoon cornstarch
1/4 teaspoon almond extract

Combine the rice, butter, salt and 1/2 cup of milk. Let stand. Prepare gelatin with water and remaining milk. Stir in almond extract. Chill until partially set. Whip cream with sugar. Fold rice mixture, cherries and whipped cream into gelatin. Spoon into an oiled 6-cup mold or casserole. Chill until set, about 4 hours. For the glaze, combine reserved cherry juice and cornstarch in a saucepan. Heat until thickened. Stir in extract. Chill. To serve, unmold fluff and drizzle with glaze. **Yield:** 6 servings.

HERBED CHICKEN

Marshall Simon, Grand Rapids, Michigan

1 tablespoon olive *or* vegetable oil
1 medium onion, chopped
1 green *or* sweet red pepper, chopped
6 large fresh mushrooms, thinly sliced

1/3 cup chicken broth
2 tablespoons red wine vinegar
1 can (29 ounces) tomato sauce
2 garlic cloves, minced
1 teaspoon sugar
1/4 teaspoon salt
1/4 teaspoon pepper
1 pound boneless skinless chicken breasts, cut into chunks
2 tablespoons chopped fresh basil *or* 1 teaspoon dried basil
1 tablespoon chopped fresh sage *or* 1/2 teaspoon dried sage
1 pound dry linguini, cooked and drained
2 to 3 tablespoons grated Parmesan cheese
2 tablespoons chopped fresh parsley

In a skillet, heat oil over medium-high. Saute onion, peppers and mushrooms until tender. Add broth and vinegar; bring to a boil. Boil 2 minutes. Add tomato sauce, garlic, sugar, salt and pepper. Bring to a boil. Reduce heat; cover and simmer 25 minutes. Add chicken, basil and sage. Cook, uncovered, 15 minutes more or until chicken is done and sauce is slightly thickened. Serve chicken and sauce over pasta. Sprinkle with cheese and parsley. **Yield:** 4 servings.

PLUM UPSIDE-DOWN CAKE

Robert Fallon, Sayville, New York

7 tablespoons butter *or* margarine, *divided*
3/4 cup sugar, *divided*
3 to 4 plums, pitted and thinly sliced
1 egg
1 cup all-purpose flour
1/4 teaspoon salt
1 teaspoon baking powder
1/3 cup milk
1 teaspoon vanilla extract

Place 1 tablespoon butter in a 9-in. round baking pan. Put pan in a preheated 350° oven to melt. Remove from oven and sprinkle with 1/3 cup sugar. Arrange plum slices in a circular pattern over sugar. Bake for 10 minutes. Meanwhile, cream the remaining butter with remaining sugar; beat in the egg. Combine flour, salt and baking powder. Add to the creamed mixture alternately with milk and vanilla, beating until smooth. Spread evenly over plums. Bake for 30 minutes or until cake tests done. Remove from the oven and immediately invert onto a large serving platter. Serve warm. **Yield:** 6-8 servings.

Celebrate Easter—or the excitement of any special occasion—by preparing the recipes on this page. They'll win compliments every time you serve them.

Start your morning with a large platter of hot Buttermilk Biscuit Sausage Pinwheels, or wait until brunch and savor the great taste of our Crab Quiche. For dinner, you'll love the garlic- and herb-laced California Roast Lamb served with fresh artichokes. Plus, leftover holiday ham quickly disappears when you prepare tasty Iowa Ham Balls.

HELP YOURSELF! Clockwise from top left: **Iowa Ham Balls, California Roast Lamb, Buttermilk Biscuit Sausage Pinwheels, Crab Quiche** (all recipes on page 38).

CHERRY CRISP

Carole Schlender, Burrton, Kansas

(PICTURED ON PAGE 31)

PASTRY:
1/4 teaspoon salt
1/2 cup packed brown sugar
1 cup all-purpose flour
1/2 cup butter *or* margarine
FILLING:
1 cup sugar
1/4 cup cornstarch
1 cup cherry juice
4 cups pitted tart red cherries
Few drops red food coloring, optional
TOPPING:
1-1/2 cups quick-cooking rolled oats
1/2 cup packed brown sugar
1/4 cup all-purpose flour
5 tablespoons butter *or*
margarine, melted

To make pastry, combine salt, brown sugar and flour in a mixing bowl. Cut in butter. Press into a 2-qt. or 11-in. x 7-in. baking dish. Bake at 350° for 15 minutes. For filling, combine sugar and cornstarch in a saucepan. Stir in juice. Cook over medium heat until thick, stirring constantly. Fold in cherries and food coloring, if desired. Pour over baked crust. Combine all topping ingredients; sprinkle over filling. Bake for 20-25 minutes or until golden brown and bubbly around edges. **Yield:** 6-8 servings.

CHERRY CREAM SCONES

Carrie Sherrill, Forestville, Wisconsin

(PICTURED ON PAGE 31)

3/4 cup dried cherries
1 cup boiling water
3 cups all-purpose flour
3 tablespoons sugar
1 tablespoon baking powder
1/2 teaspoon salt
1/2 teaspoon cream of tartar
1/2 cup butter, room temperature
1 egg, *separated*
1/2 cup sour cream
3/4 cup half-and-half cream
1-1/2 teaspoons almond extract
Additional sugar

Soak cherries in water for 10 minutes. Drain and set aside. In a large mixing bowl, combine the flour, sugar, baking powder, salt and cream of tartar. With a pastry blender, cut in the butter. Set aside. In a small bowl, combine egg yolk, sour cream, half-and-half and extract. Add to flour mixture; stir until a soft dough forms. Turn out onto a lightly floured surface; knead gently six to

eight times. Knead in cherries. Divide dough in half and shape into balls. Roll each ball into a 6-in. circle. Cut into six wedges. Repeat with remaining ball. Place on lightly greased baking sheet. Beat the egg white until foamy; brush tops of scones and sprinkle with sugar. Bake at 400° for 15-20 minutes. Serve warm. **Yield:** 12 scones.

CHERRY CHEESECAKE TARTS

Mary Lindell, Sanford, Michigan

(PICTURED ON PAGE 31)

1 package (10 ounces) frozen puff pastry shells
2 packages (3 ounces *each*) cream cheese, softened
1/4 cup confectioners' sugar
1/2 teaspoon almond extract
1 can (21 ounces) cherry pie filling
Additional confectioners' sugar

Bake pastry shells according to package directions. Meanwhile, in a mixing bowl, beat cream cheese, sugar and extract. With a fork, carefully remove the circular top of each baked shell and set aside. Remove any soft layers of pastry inside shells and discard. Divide the cheese filling among the shells; place on a baking sheet. Return to the oven and bake 5 minutes. Cool. Just before serving, fill each shell with pie filling. Top with reserved pastry circles. Dust with additional confectioners' sugar. **Yield:** 6 servings.

CHERRY/RHUBARB COBBLER

Mary Ann Earnest, Effingham, Illinois

(PICTURED ON PAGE 31)

FILLING:
1 can (21 ounces) cherry pie filling
3 cups chopped rhubarb
1 cup sugar
4 tablespoons butter *or* margarine
CRUST:
1/2 cup shortening
1 cup sugar
1 egg
1 cup all-purpose flour
1 teaspoon baking powder
1/2 cup milk

Spread fruit in a 13-in. x 9-in. x 2-in. baking pan. Sprinkle with sugar and dot with butter. For crust, cream short-

ening and sugar in a mixing bowl. Add egg and beat well. Set aside. Combine flour and baking powder; add alternately with milk to creamed mixture. Pour over fruit; bake at 350° for 50-60 minutes. **Yield:** about 12 servings.

NORTHWEST CHERRY SALSA

Margaret Slocum, Ridgefield, Washington

(PICTURED ON PAGE 32)

✓ This tasty dish uses less sugar, salt and fat. Recipe includes *Diabetic Exchanges*.

1 cup fresh *or* frozen pitted dark sweet cherries, chopped
2 tablespoons chopped fresh basil
1 tablespoon finely chopped green pepper
1 teaspoon lemon juice
1/4 teaspoon Worcestershire sauce
1/4 teaspoon grated lemon peel
1/8 teaspoon salt
Dash hot pepper sauce

Combine all ingredients; refrigerate at least 1 hour. Serve as a condiment with chicken, turkey or pork. **Yield:** 3/4 cup. **Diabetic Exchanges:** One serving (2 tablespoons) equals 1/2 fruit; also, 22 calories, 59 mg sodium, 0 mg cholesterol, 5 gm carbohydrate, 1 gm protein, 1/2 gm fat.

CREAMY CHERRY CHEESECAKE

Julie Sibley, Kenai, Alaska

(PICTURED ON PAGE 32)

CRUST:
1-1/2 cups graham cracker crumbs (21 squares)
1/4 cup sugar
6 tablespoons butter *or* margarine, melted
FILLING:
2 packages (8 ounces *each*) cream cheese, softened
2 eggs
1/2 cup sugar
1 teaspoon vanilla extract
SOUR CREAM TOPPING:
1 cup (8 ounces) sour cream
1/4 cup sugar
1 teaspoon vanilla extract
CHERRY TOPPING:
1/2 cup sugar
2 tablespoons cornstarch
1 can (16 ounces) pitted tart red

cherries, juice drained and reserved
1 teaspoon lemon juice
Few drops red food coloring

Combine all crust ingredients. Press onto the bottom and one-third the way up the sides of a 9-in. springform pan. Set aside. For filling, beat cream cheese until smooth. Add eggs, sugar and vanilla; beat until smooth. Pour into prepared crust. Bake at 375° for 20 minutes. Remove from oven; cool 15 minutes. Meanwhile, combine all sour cream topping ingredients. Spread over filling. Bake at 400° for 10 minutes. Cool to room temperature; cover and chill 10-12 hours. For cherry topping, combine sugar and cornstarch in a saucepan; blend in the cherry juice. Heat, stirring constantly, until thickened. Remove from heat; stir in lemon juice, food coloring and cherries. Cool 5 minutes. Spread on top of cheesecake; chill 2 hours. **Yield:** 10 servings.

CHERRY/ALMOND HAM GLAZE

Julie Sterchi, Fairfield, Illinois

(PICTURED ON PAGE 32)

1 jar (12 ounces) cherry preserves
1/4 cup vinegar
2 tablespoons corn syrup
1/4 teaspoon ground cinnamon
1/4 teaspoon ground cloves
1/4 teaspoon ground nutmeg
1/3 cup slivered almonds
3 tablespoons water

In a saucepan, combine all ingredients except almonds and water. Bring to a boil. Reduce heat; simmer 2 minutes, stirring frequently. Stir in the almonds. About 15 minutes before ham is done, spoon 1/4 to 1/3 cup glaze over ham. Repeat if desired. Stir water into remaining glaze; heat through and serve with ham. **Yield:** about 1-1/2 cups.

CHERRY/NUT BREAKFAST ROLLS

Darlene Markel, Roseburg, Oregon

(PICTURED ON PAGE 33)

2 packages (1/4 ounce each) active dry yeast
1 cup warm water (110°-115°)
1/2 cup butter or margarine, melted
1/2 cup sugar
3 eggs, beaten
1/2 teaspoon salt

4-1/2 to 5 cups all-purpose flour, *divided*
FILLING:
3 cups fresh *or* frozen pitted tart red cherries, chopped
2/3 cup sugar
3 tablespoons cornstarch
1/4 teaspoon almond extract
1/3 cup finely chopped almonds
Few drops red food coloring, optional
ICING:
1/2 cup confectioners' sugar
1/2 to 2 teaspoons milk
1/2 teaspoon softened butter *or* margarine
1/2 teaspoon almond extract

In a large mixing bowl, dissolve yeast in water. Let stand 5 minutes. Stir in butter, sugar, eggs, salt and 3 cups flour. Add enough remaining flour to form a soft dough. Turn out onto a floured surface; knead until smooth and elastic, about 6-8 minutes. Place dough in a greased bowl, turning once to grease top. Cover and refrigerate 2 hours. Meanwhile, combine all filling ingredients in a saucepan. Bring to a boil; reduce heat and cook until thickened, stirring constantly. Cool. Turn dough out onto a lightly floured surface. Roll out to make a 14-in. x 16-in. rectangle. Spread with filling. Roll up, jelly-roll style, beginning with the long end. Cut into 12 slices. Place, cut side down, on a greased 13-in. x 9-in. x 2-in. baking pan. Cover and let rise until almost doubled, about 25 minutes. Bake at 375° for 25 minutes or until golden brown. Remove from pan; cool slightly. Combine all icing ingredients; drizzle over warm rolls. Serve immediately. **Yield:** 12 rolls.

CHERRY CHEWBILEES

Debbi Smith, Crossett, Arkansas

(PICTURED ON PAGE 33)

CRUST:
1-1/4 cups all-purpose flour
1/2 cup packed brown sugar
1/2 cup butter-flavored shortening
1 cup chopped walnuts, *divided*
1/2 cup flaked coconut
FILLING:
2 packages (8 ounces each) cream cheese, softened
2/3 cup sugar
2 eggs
2 teaspoons vanilla extract
2 cans (21 ounces each) cherry pie filling

In a bowl, combine flour and brown sugar; cut in shortening until fine crumbs form. Stir in 1/2 cup nuts and coconut. Reserve 1/2 cup crumb mixture for top-

ping. Press remaining mixture into the bottom of a greased 13-in. x 9-in. x 2-in. baking pan. Bake at 350° for 12-15 minutes or until lightly browned. Meanwhile, for filling, beat cream cheese, sugar, eggs and vanilla in a mixing bowl until smooth. Spread over the hot crust. Bake 15 minutes. Spread pie filling on top. Combine remaining nuts and reserved crumbs; sprinkle over cherries. Bake 15 minutes more. Cool. Refrigerate until serving. **Yield:** 20 servings.

EASY CHERRY FRUIT SOUP

Virginia Shellum, Nicollet, Minnesota

(PICTURED ON PAGE 33)

1 can (21 ounces) cherry pie filling
1 can (8 ounces) pineapple chunks in natural juices, undrained
2 cups water
2/3 cup chopped dried apricots
1 cup pitted prunes
1 tablespoon butter *or* margarine
2 lemon slices
1 teaspoon quick-cooking tapioca

In a 3-qt. casserole, combine all ingredients. Cover and bake at 325° for 1 hour. Serve warm. **Yield:** 6-8 servings.

CHERRY CINNAMON DESSERT RING

Catherine Aitken, Courtenay, British Columbia

(PICTURED ON PAGE 33)

3 cups fresh *or* frozen pitted dark sweet cherries
3-1/4 cups water, *divided*
1 cup sugar
2 cinnamon sticks
1 teaspoon almond extract
2 envelopes unflavored gelatin
Sweetened whipped cream

In a saucepan, combine cherries with 3 cups of water, sugar and cinnamon. Bring to a boil; reduce heat, cover and simmer 15 minutes. Remove from the heat. Remove cinnamon sticks and stir in extract. Set aside. Place remaining water in a saucepan. Sprinkle gelatin over water; let stand 1 minute. Heat until dissolved. Stir into cherry mixture and mix well. Refrigerate until mixture begins to thicken, stirring occasionally to distribute cherries evenly. Spoon into a 5-1/2-cup ring mold. Refrigerate until set, about 3-4 hours. Turn onto a serving platter. Serve with whipped cream. **Yield:** 20 servings.

DEEP-DISH CHERRY PIE

Lillian Heston, Warren, New Jersey

(PICTURED ON PAGE 33)

6 cups pitted tart red cherries
3/4 cup sugar
3/4 cup packed brown sugar
3 tablespoons cornstarch
1 teaspoon almond extract
Few drops red food coloring, optional
Dash salt
3 to 4 tablespoons butter or margarine
CRUST:
1-1/2 cups all-purpose flour
1 tablespoon sugar
1/2 teaspoon salt
1/2 teaspoon ground nutmeg
1/2 cup plus 2 tablespoons shortening
4 to 5 tablespoons ice water
Milk or cream
Additional sugar

In a large mixing bowl, combine cherries, sugars, cornstarch, extract, food coloring and salt. Place in a greased 1-1/2-qt. to 2-qt. casserole. Dot with butter. Set aside. For crust, combine flour, sugar, salt and nutmeg. Cut in shortening. Add water, a little at a time, until a dough forms. Do not overmix. Roll out on a floured surface to fit the top of the casserole. Place on top of the cherries, pressing against the sides of the dish. Cut decorative designs or slits in center of crust. Brush with milk or cream and sprinkle with sugar. Bake at 350° for 1 hour or until crust is golden brown. Cool at least 15 minutes before serving. **Yield:** 8-10 servings.

IOWA HAM BALLS

Helen Koehler, Liscomb, Iowa

(PICTURED ON PAGE 35)

3-1/2 pounds ground ham
1-1/2 pounds ground beef
3 eggs, beaten
2 cups milk
3 cups graham cracker crumbs
2 cans (10-3/4 ounces each) condensed tomato soup, undiluted
3/4 cup vinegar
2-1/2 cups packed brown sugar
1 teaspoon prepared mustard

In a large mixing bowl, combine first five ingredients. Using a 1/3 cup measure, shape mixture into 2-in. balls. Place in two large shallow roasting pans. Combine all remaining ingredients; pour over balls. Bake at 325° for 1 hour, basting frequently with sauce. **Yield:** about 15 servings.

GRANDMA'S OATMEAL BREAD

Marcia Hostetter, Ogdensburg, New York

1-1/2 cups boiling water
1 tablespoon butter or margarine
2 teaspoons salt
1/2 cup sugar
1 cup rolled oats
2 packages (1/4 ounce each) active dry yeast
3/4 cup warm water (110°-115°)
1/4 cup molasses
1/4 cup packed brown sugar
6 to 6-1/2 cups all-purpose flour, divided

In a small mixing bowl, combine boiling water, butter, salt and sugar. Stir in oats; cool to lukewarm. In a large mixing bowl, dissolve yeast in warm water. Stir in molasses, brown sugar and 1 cup flour. Beat until smooth. Add oat mixture and enough remaining flour to make a stiff dough. Turn out onto a floured board; knead until smooth and elastic, about 6-8 minutes. Shape into a ball. Place in a greased bowl, turning once to grease top. Cover and allow to rise until doubled, about 1-1/2 hours. Punch dough down; divide in half and shape into balls. Cover and let rest 10 minutes. Shape into loaves and place into two greased 9-in. x 5-in. x 3-in. loaf pans. Cover and let rise until nearly doubled, about 1 hour. Bake at 375° for 35 minutes. Cover loosely with foil the last 20 minutes if loaves are browning excessively. Remove from pans and cool on wire rack. **Yield:** 2 loaves.

CALIFORNIA ROAST LAMB

Ann Eastman, Greenville, California

(PICTURED ON PAGE 35)

1 leg of lamb (4 to 5 pounds)
2 to 3 garlic cloves, halved
1 teaspoon seasoned salt
1 teaspoon pepper
1 teaspoon dried oregano
2 cans (8 ounces each) tomato sauce
1 cup water
Juice of 1 lemon
3 to 5 large fresh artichokes, quartered
Fresh lemon slices

Cut slits in lamb; insert garlic. Rub meat with salt, pepper and oregano. Roast at 400° for 30 minutes. Reduce heat to 350°; roast 1 hour more. Skim off any fat in pan; pour tomato sauce, water and lemon juice over lamb. Place artichokes around meat. Roast 1 hour longer or to desired doneness, basting occasionally with pan juices. Garnish with lemon. **Yield:** 10-12 servings.

BUTTERMILK BISCUIT SAUSAGE PINWHEELS

Gladys Ferguson, Rossville, Georgia

(PICTURED ON PAGE 35)

1/4 cup shortening
2 cups unsifted self-rising flour
1 cup buttermilk
1 pound raw bulk pork sausage, room temperature

With a pastry blender, cut shortening into flour. Add buttermilk; mix. On a lightly floured board, knead for a few seconds, adding additional flour if necessary. Roll out onto a lightly floured board into a 12-in. x 9-in. rectangle. Spread sausage over dough. Roll up, jelly-roll style, starting from the short side. Chill. Cut into 1/2-in. slices. Place, cut side down, on a lightly greased baking sheet. Bake at 425° for 25 minutes or until lightly browned. **Yield:** about 9 servings.

CRAB QUICHE

Michele Field, Burtonsville, Maryland

(PICTURED ON PAGE 35)

1/2 cup mayonnaise
2 tablespoons all-purpose flour
2 eggs, beaten
1/2 cup milk
2 cans (6 ounces each) flaked crabmeat, drained
1/3 cup chopped green onions
1 tablespoon finely chopped parsley
2 cups (8 ounces) shredded Swiss cheese
1 unbaked pastry shell (9 inches)

In a mixing bowl, combine mayonnaise, flour, eggs and milk. Stir in crab, onions, parsley and cheese. Spoon into the pastry shell. Bake at 350° for 1 hour. **Yield:** 6-8 servings.

EASY AS PIE: If you find it difficult to put your pie crust into your pie pan, simply roll the dough back onto your rolling pin. Then just put it over the pan, unroll it and shape into the pan.

BROCCOLI/CHEESE TWICE-BAKED POTATOES

Joyce Brown, Genesee, Idaho

6 medium baking potatoes
1/2 cup sour cream
3 tablespoons butter *or*
 margarine
1/2 teaspoon salt
1/4 teaspoon pepper
2 green onions, thinly sliced
1-1/2 cups cooked chopped broccoli
1 cup (4 ounces) shredded
 cheddar cheese, *divided*
Paprika

Bake potatoes at 425° for 45-60 minutes or until soft. Cut a lengthwise slice from the top of the potatoes. Scoop out pulp and place in bowl. Mash potatoes; add sour cream, butter, salt, pepper, onions, broccoli and 3/4 cup cheese. Refill potato shells; top with remaining cheese and sprinkle with paprika. Bake at 425° for 20-25 minutes or until heated through. **Yield:** 6 servings.

STRAWBERRY CREAM CAKE ROLL

Laura Hagedorn, Fort Branch, Indiana

4 eggs
1 teaspoon vanilla extract
3/4 cup sugar
3/4 cup sifted cake flour
1 teaspoon baking powder
1/4 teaspoon salt
Confectioners' sugar
CREAM FILLING:
1 cup whipping cream
1/4 cup sugar
1/2 teaspoon vanilla extract
2 cups fresh *or* frozen
 strawberries, cut up
Confectioners' sugar
Additional whole strawberries
Whipped cream, optional

In a mixing bowl, beat eggs with vanilla on high speed with an electric mixer for 5 minutes or until lemon-colored. Gradually add sugar, beating until dissolved. Combine flour, baking powder and salt; fold gently into egg mixture just until combined. Pour into a greased and waxed paper-lined jelly roll pan. Spread batter evenly over pan. Bake at 375° for 10-12 minutes or until light brown. Turn out onto a cloth that has been sprinkled with confectioners' sugar. Peel off paper from cake; roll up cloth and cake. Cool. For filling, whip cream, sugar and vanilla. Unroll cake and spread filling over it; sprinkle with strawberries. Roll up the cake again

and chill 2 hours before serving. Sprinkle with confectioners' sugar; garnish with strawberries, and additional whipped cream if desired. **Yield:** 10 servings.

ORANGE PECAN MUFFINS

Margie Schwartz, Sarasota, Florida

1-1/4 cups all-purpose flour
1 teaspoon salt
1-1/2 teaspoons baking soda
3/4 cup sugar
4 large oranges
Water
2 eggs, beaten
1/2 cup vegetable oil
4-1/2 cups raisin bran cereal
1 cup chopped pecans

In a large mixing bowl, combine first four ingredients. Set aside. Remove the peel from two of the oranges. Cut all the oranges into eighths and remove seeds; puree in a blender or food processor. If necessary, add enough water to puree to equal 2 cups. Stir oranges, eggs, oil, cereal and pecans into the dry ingredients. Blend only until mixed. Fill greased muffin tins 3/4 full. Bake at 375° for 20-25 minutes. **Yield:** 18 muffins.

CAULIFLOWER CHEESE SOUP

Mrs. Dave Barba, Downers Grove, Illinois

1/4 cup water
2 tablespoons butter *or*
 margarine
1/2 cup shredded carrots
1/4 cup chopped onion
2 cans (10-3/4 ounces *each*)
 condensed cream of potato
 soup, undiluted
2 cups milk
1 can (7 ounces) whole kernel
 corn, drained
1 to 2 cups fresh *or* frozen
 cauliflower florets, cooked
 just until tender

1 cup (4 ounces) shredded
 cheddar cheese
1/2 cup shredded Provolone *or*
 mozzarella cheese
1/8 teaspoon pepper

In a saucepan, heat first four ingredients until carrots are tender. Stir in soup, milk, corn and cauliflower. Heat through. Just before serving, stir in the cheeses and pepper. Serve immediately. **Yield:** 6-8 servings.

RHUBARB COFFEE CAKE

Genelle Andrews, South Roxana, Illinois

1-1/2 cups packed brown sugar
1/2 cup shortening
1 egg
2 cups all-purpose flour
1 teaspoon baking soda
1/2 teaspoon salt
1 cup (8 ounces) sour cream
1-1/2 cups chopped rhubarb
TOPPING:
1/4 cup sugar
1/4 cup packed brown sugar
1/2 cup chopped pecans *or*
 walnuts
1 tablespoon butter *or*
 margarine
1 teaspoon ground cinnamon

In a mixing bowl, cream brown sugar and shortening. Add egg. Combine flour, baking soda and salt; add alternately with sour cream to the brown sugar/shortening mixture. Fold in rhubarb. Spread in a greased 13-in. x 9-in. x 2-in. baking pan. Combine all topping ingredients; sprinkle over batter. Bake at 350° for 45-50 minutes. Cool on wire rack. **Yield:** about 12 servings.

COUNTRY CHEESE SNACKS

Sandy Thorn, Sonora, California

1 cup mayonnaise
1 cup grated Parmesan cheese
1 package (8 ounces) cream
 cheese, softened
2 green onions with tops,
 minced
Snack-size rye bread slices *or*
 toasted English muffins *or* bagels
Parsley sprigs
Stuffed green olives, sliced

In a small bowl, combine first four ingredients. Spread on bread; place on a baking sheet. Broil 4 in. from the heat until golden and bubbly, about 1-2 minutes. Garnish with parsley and olives. Serve immediately. **Yield:** 2 cups spread.

'My Most Memorable Meal'

The savory smells and tantalizing tastes of a wonderful meal can bring back a surge of magical memories. Marion Kirst of Troy, Michigan harks back to the care-free summers of her childhood each time she prepares the bountiful breakfast that her Aunt Edith served during the late 1930's.

"When school let out in the spring, my younger brother and I would get to spend a week at Aunt Edith and Uncle Tom's in Chicago," Marion recalls fondly.

"The week always ended too soon, and our parents would arrive on Saturday evening to take us back home on Sunday," Marion says. "To send us on our way, Aunt Edith made a mighty breakfast that I've never forgotten.

"I still use Aunt Edith's recipes —especially for brunches. They always bring back happy memories of my kind and generous aunt and uncle. They opened new worlds to us and provided us with fond memories that will be with us forever."

BOUNTIFUL BREAKFAST. Clockwise from top right: **Strawberry Muffins, Fresh Fruit Bowl, Night-Before Casserole, Aunt Edith's Baked Pancake** (all recipes on page 41).

MEMORABLE MEAL

The first four recipes listed here come from Marion Kirst of Troy, Michigan (see photo and story at left).

STRAWBERRY MUFFINS

2 cups all-purpose flour
1 cup sugar
1 teaspoon baking soda
1 teaspoon ground cinnamon
1 teaspoon ground nutmeg
1/2 teaspoon salt
2 eggs, beaten
1/2 cup vegetable oil
1/2 cup buttermilk
1/2 cup strawberry jam

In a mixing bowl, stir together flour, sugar, baking soda, cinnamon, nutmeg and salt; make a well in the center. Combine eggs, oil and buttermilk; pour all at once into the well. Stir just until dry ingredients are moistened. Do not overmix. Gently fold in jam (a few lumps will remain). Place in well-greased or paper-lined muffin tins. Bake at 375° for 20 minutes. **Yield:** 18 muffins.

NIGHT-BEFORE CASSEROLE

12 slices white bread, crusts removed
6 to 8 tablespoons butter *or* margarine, softened
6 slices deluxe American cheese
6 slices boiled *or* baked ham
Prepared mustard
4 eggs, beaten
3 cups milk
Chopped fresh parsley
MUSHROOM SAUCE:
1 can (10-3/4 ounces) cream of mushroom soup, undiluted
1/3 cup milk
Dash Worcestershire sauce

Spread bread with butter. Place six slices, buttered side up, in the bottom of a greased 13-in. x 9-in. x 2-in. bak-

ing pan. Top each bread slice with a slice of cheese and ham. Brush with mustard. Place the remaining bread slices, buttered side up, over mustard. Beat eggs and milk; pour over all. Cover and refrigerate overnight. Bake at 300° for 1 hour. Let stand 5 minutes before serving. Meanwhile, heat sauce ingredients and keep warm. To serve, garnish casserole with parsley and pass the mushroom sauce. **Yield:** 12 servings.

FRESH FRUIT BOWL

8 to 10 cups fresh melon cubes
1 to 2 tablespoons white corn syrup
1 pint fresh strawberries
2 cups fresh pineapple chunks
2 oranges, sectioned
Fresh mint leaves, optional

In a large bowl, combine melon cubes and corn syrup. Cover and refrigerate overnight. Just before serving, stir in remaining fruit. Garnish with fresh mint leaves if desired. **Yield:** 3-4 quarts.

AUNT EDITH'S BAKED PANCAKE

3 eggs
1/2 teaspoon salt
1/2 cup all-purpose flour
1/2 cup milk
2 tablespoons butter *or* margarine, softened
Confectioners' sugar
Lemon wedges

In a mixing bowl, beat eggs until very light. Add salt, flour and milk; beat well. Thoroughly rub bottom and sides of a 10-in. cast-iron or heavy skillet with butter. Pour batter into skillet. Bake at 450° for 15 minutes. Reduce heat to 350° and bake 5 minutes more or until set. Remove pancake from skillet and place on a large hot platter. Dust with confectioners' sugar and garnish with lemon. Serve immediately. **Yield:** 4-6 servings.

CHICKEN PAPRIKASH WITH SPAETZLE

John Niklasch, Terre Haute, Indiana

4 tablespoons butter *or* margarine
1 jar (16 ounces) whole onions, drained
1 large onion, chopped
1/2 cup all-purpose flour
2 tablespoons paprika, *divided*

1 broiler/fryer chicken (2-1/2 to 3 pounds), cut up
1/2 teaspoon salt
3 tablespoons chopped fresh parsley
1-1/4 cups chicken broth
1 cup (8 ounces) sour cream
3 tablespoons capers with juice
SPAETZLE:
2 eggs, well beaten
1-1/2 cups all-purpose flour
1/2 cup milk
3/4 teaspoon salt
1/4 teaspoon baking powder
1 tablespoon butter *or* margarine

In a heavy skillet, melt butter over medium-high heat. Saute whole onions until lightly browned. Remove and set aside. Saute chopped onion until tender. Set aside. Combine flour and 1-1/2 teaspoons paprika in a plastic bag. Place several chicken parts in flour mixture; shake to coat. Repeat until all chicken has been coated. Place chicken in skillet; brown on all sides. Add salt, parsley, broth and remaining paprika. Cover and cook over low heat until chicken is tender, about 45 minutes. Meanwhile, for spaetzle, bring a large kettle of salted water to a boil. Combine eggs, flour, milk, salt and baking powder. With a spoon, drop small dumplings into water. Reduce heat and simmer, covered, 10 minutes. Drain spaetzle and toss with butter. Remove chicken from skillet; stir in sour cream, capers with juice and onions. Return chicken to the skillet and gently heat through. Place spaetzle on a platter and top with chicken. Ladle the sauce over all. **Yield:** 6-8 servings. *Editor's Note:* Boneless veal, cut into strips, may be substituted for the chicken.

CONGO SQUARES

Darlene Cook, Mustang, Oklahoma

2/3 cup shortening
2-1/4 cups packed brown sugar
2-3/4 cups all-purpose flour
2-1/2 teaspoons baking powder
1/2 teaspoon salt
3 eggs, beaten
1 tablespoon vanilla extract
2 cups (12 ounces) semisweet chocolate chips
1 cup chopped nuts

In a saucepan, melt shortening over medium heat. Stir in brown sugar. Cool slightly. Combine flour, baking powder and salt; add gradually with eggs to shortening mixture. Stir in the vanilla, chips and nuts (batter will be very stiff). Spread into a greased and floured 12-in. x 9-in. x 2-in. baking pan. Bake at 350° for 25-30 minutes. Cut into squares while warm. **Yield:** about 48 bars.

Pull up a chair, and dig into these delightful dishes with your family. Start with buttery chicken that's been dipped in bread crumbs and baked to a golden brown. Serve it alongside hearty helpings of coleslaw, and finish up with slices of light and airy Hot Milk Cake made in your well-seasoned cast-iron skillet.

DOWN-HOME DINNER. Top to bottom: Hot Milk Cake, Pennsylvania Dutch Coleslaw, Marie's Chicken Bake (all recipes on page 49).

MEALS IN MINUTES

AS a home economics teacher, she helps others learn to make the most of minutes in the kitchen. And, with a growing family of her own, Nancy Brown of Janesville, Wisconsin has plenty of practical experience!

"The secret is planning," Nancy notes. "On weekends, I work out the menus for the week ahead...and often I roast a chicken or ham so I'll have leftovers for quick meals later."

A little leftover ham makes a fast, filling meal when she prepares her Ham and Cheese Frittata, featured below. "The recipe is flexible," Nancy assures. "In summer, I frequently add fresh herbs and zucchini."

Gardening's a favorite activity for Nancy, who counts herself lucky to have the summers off to enjoy it. Her home is always decorated with bouquets of fresh flowers, plus Nancy dries flowers and herbs for basket arrangements and wreaths.

An afternoon gardening or crafting still leaves time for this 30-minute meal, however. "Fresh tomatoes add a flavorful touch, and the dessert can include fruit in season," she advises. "Kids just love that treat."

Likely, you'll love Nancy's menu, too. It might even leave *you* more time for gardening!

HAM AND CHEESE FRITTATA

  2 tablespoons butter *or* **margarine**
1/2 cup sliced fresh mushrooms
1/2 cup chopped sweet red *or* **green pepper**
1/4 cup sliced green onions
  6 eggs
  2 tablespoons water
1/2 cup diced cooked ham
  1 cup (4 ounces) shredded cheddar cheese

In a skillet, melt butter over medium heat. Saute mushrooms, pepper and onions until tender. In a mixing bowl, beat eggs with water until foamy; stir in ham. Pour over the vegetables. Let eggs set on the bottom, then lift the edges to allow any uncooked egg to flow underneath. Cover and cook until the eggs are set, about 3 minutes. Sprinkle with cheese and cut into wedges to serve. **Yield:** 4 servings.

PARMESAN TOMATOES

  2 large tomatoes
  3 tablespoons dry bread crumbs
  2 tablespoons grated Parmesan cheese
  2 tablespoons butter *or* **margarine, melted**
1/2 teaspoon dried basil *or* **1 tablespoon snipped fresh basil**
1/2 teaspoon chopped fresh parsley
Dash pepper

Remove stems from the tomatoes and halve crosswise. Place, cut side up, in a small baking dish. Combine all remaining ingredients; sprinkle over tomato tops. Bake at 375° for 15 minutes or until heated through. **Yield:** 4 servings.

GLAZED FRUIT DESSERT

  1 package (3.4 ounces) instant vanilla pudding mix
  1 can (20 ounces) pineapple chunks in natural juice, liquid drained and reserved
  1 can (11 ounces) mandarin oranges, drained
  2 bananas, sliced
Whipped topping

In a mixing bowl, combine pudding and pineapple juice. Stir until thickened. Fold in pineapple, oranges and bananas. Refrigerate until serving. Garnish with a dollop of whipped topping. **Yield:** 6 servings.

Quick & Easy Squash/Zucchini

READY FOR the speedy spread of squash in your garden? These quick delicious recipes will help you make the most of those prolific palate-pleasing vegetables!

CANDIED ACORN SQUASH RINGS

Rita Addicks, Weimar, Texas

2 acorn squash, cut into 1-inch rings and seeded
2/3 cup packed brown sugar
1/2 cup butter *or* margarine, softened

Arrange squash in a shallow baking pan; cover with foil. Bake at 350° for 35-40 minutes or until tender. Combine sugar and butter; spread over squash. Bake, uncovered, for 15-20 minutes, basting occasionally. **Yield:** 6 servings.

YELLOW SQUASH CASSEROLE

Mae Kruis, Gallup, New Mexico

3 tablespoons butter *or* margarine
3 to 4 yellow summer squash, sliced
1 medium onion, chopped
1 can (4 ounces) chopped green chilies
8 to 10 saltine crackers, crushed

RINGS WITH ZING (recipe above) require just three ingredients, an hour or less to bake.

Salt and pepper to taste
1-1/2 cups (6 ounces) shredded cheddar cheese

In a skillet, melt butter over medium-high heat. Saute squash and onion until crisp-tender. Remove from the heat; stir in chilies, crackers, salt and pepper. Spoon into a greased 1-1/2-qt. casserole. Top with cheese. Bake at 350° for 15-20 minutes. **Yield:** 4-6 servings.

RATATOUILLE

Donna Rushing, Belk, Alabama

3 tablespoons olive *or* vegetable oil
3 medium zucchini, cut into 1/2-inch slices
2 large tomatoes, peeled and chopped
1 large onion, chopped
1 green pepper, cut into strips
1/4 cup minced fresh parsley
1 tablespoon minced fresh basil *or* 1 teaspoon dried basil
1/2 teaspoon salt
1/4 teaspoon pepper

In a large Dutch oven, heat oil over medium-high. Saute all ingredients for 5 minutes. Cover and simmer, stirring occasionally, 15 minutes or until vegetables are tender. **Yield:** 6-8 servings.

WINTER SQUASH CHEESE CASSEROLE

Alberta Goodrich, Portland, Connecticut

2 pounds winter squash, peeled, seeded and cut into 1-inch cubes
1 tablespoon butter *or* margarine
1/2 cup chopped onion
2 cups (8 ounces) shredded cheddar cheese, *divided*
2 eggs
3/4 cup milk
Salt and pepper to taste
1/2 cup soft bread crumbs
Ground nutmeg to taste

In a saucepan, cook squash in enough water to cover until tender. Drain. In a skillet, melt butter over medium-high heat. Saute onion until tender. Place squash in a greased 2-qt. casserole.

Top with the onion and half the cheese. Beat the eggs, milk and seasonings together. Pour over the squash. Top with remaining cheese; sprinkle with bread crumbs and nutmeg. Bake at 325° for 30 minutes or until set and lightly browned. Serve immediately. **Yield:** 8 servings.

ZUCCHINI/OATMEAL MUFFINS

Janet Bonarski, Perry, New York

2-1/2 cups all-purpose flour
1-1/2 cups sugar
1 cup chopped pecans
1/2 cup quick-cooking oats
1 tablespoon baking powder
1 teaspoon salt
1 teaspoon ground cinnamon
4 eggs
1 medium zucchini, shredded (about 3/4 cup)
3/4 cup vegetable oil

In a mixing bowl, combine first seven ingredients. Beat eggs; combine with zucchini and oil. Pour over dry ingredients, stirring only until moistened. Batter will be lumpy. Fill greased muffin cups 3/4 full. Bake at 400° for 25 minutes or until a toothpick inserted in the center comes out clean. Cool on wire rack. **Yield:** 1 dozen.

STUFFED ZUCCHINI

Vonnie Elledge, Pinole, California

4 medium zucchini squash
2 tablespoons cooking oil
1 small onion, minced
2 eggs, lightly beaten
1/2 cup dry bread crumbs
1/4 cup grated Parmesan cheese
2 tablespoons minced parsley
Salt and pepper to taste

Cut zucchini in half lengthwise. Scoop out pulp, leaving a 3/8-in. shell. Reserve pulp. Parboil shells in salted water 2 minutes. Remove and drain. Set aside. Chop zucchini pulp. In a skillet, heat oil over medium-high. Saute the onion and chopped zucchini until tender. Remove from the heat and combine remaining ingredients. Fill shells. Place in a greased baking dish. Bake at 375° for 15 minutes or until heated through. **Yield:** 8 servings.

Too much of a good thing—that's what an annual abundance of squash seems to bring…and bring …and *bring*.

What's a country cook to do? Turn to the delicious dishes here and on the next two pages to solve your squash surplus in all sorts of flavorful new ways—from a(corn) to z(ucchini). So start cooking… and turn "excess" into "exciting" at your table!

GOURDGEOUS! Clockwise from top: **Cheddar/Squash Cloverleaf Rolls** (p. 49), **Squash-Stuffed Chicken** (p. 49), **Butternut Apple Crisp** (p. 49), **Marinated Zucchini Salad** (p. 50).

Hearty, healthful squash isn't just for autumn anymore. It's popping up in plenty of savory recipes the whole family can enjoy year-round...from crispy fritters and a palate-pleasing pie to a simple-to-make casserole and a tasty stir-fry.

GOOD AND PLENTY. Clockwise from lower left: **Zucchini/Herb Pate** (p. 50), **Confetti Zucchini Relish** (p. 50), **Spaghetti Squash Casserole** (p. 50), **Zucchini Fritters** (p. 50), **Squash Custard Pie** (p. 50), **Winter Squash Squares** (p. 52), **Garden Harvest Chili** (p. 52), **Squash and Broccoli Stir-Fry** (p. 52).

MEALS IN MINUTES

TWO busy youngsters and a split-shift job as a waitress leave Denise Blackman little time on weeknights for making the meals she serves her own family. That's why Denise counts on a helpful husband…and on Meals in Minutes menus!

"With my changeable work schedule and our children's many activities, I need recipes that are quick to fix and easy enough for my husband to prepare when I have to work in the evening," declares Denise.

Fast doesn't rule out fresh ingredients, however. Denise prefers using them whenever possible. And, on weekends, when life is a little less hectic for the Blackmans, she loves to cook more complicated dishes and have fun with fancy desserts besides.

The meal pictured here is a summer favorite with the Blackman family. It features fresh salmon—a seafood that's a mealtime mainstay in Denise's home area of Port Cartier, Quebec. (If fresh salmon isn't readily available where you live, Denise assures other fish varieties will also work well.)

Enjoy summer's garden greens in a crisp salad crowned with creamy blue cheese dressing. And take advantage of plentiful seasonal squash and tiny red potatoes for the speedy and delicious vegetable side dish.

But be sure to save room for dessert —fresh berries topped with a dollop of orangy whipped cream are a perfect ending to an extra-easy meal that goes from start to finish in a flash!

FISH FILLETS IN GARLIC BUTTER

- 2 tablespoons butter *or* margarine
- 2 small garlic cloves, minced
- 4 fish fillets (about 6 ounces *each*) salmon (*or* whitefish *or* cod)
- 1/4 cup thinly sliced green onion
Lemon wedges

In a skillet, melt butter over medium heat. Saute garlic 1 minute. Place fish over garlic, cover and cook over low heat 3 minutes. Carefully turn fish; sprinkle with onions. Cover and continue to cook until fish flakes easily with a fork, about 2-3 minutes. Squeeze lemon over fish. Serve immediately. **Yield:** 4 servings.

BLUE CHEESE DRESSING

- 1/4 cup crumbled blue cheese
- 3/4 cup sour cream, *divided*
- 2 tablespoons vegetable oil
- 1 tablespoon lemon juice
- 1 to 1-1/2 teaspoons Worcestershire sauce, optional
Salt and pepper to taste

In a small bowl, mash blue cheese with a fork. Add 2 tablespoons sour cream; beat until smooth. Stir in all remaining ingredients. Serve over mixed greens. **Yield:** 1 cup.

SUMMER SQUASH AND POTATO SAUTE

- 2 tablespoons butter *or* margarine
- 2 medium summer squash, sliced
- 2 small red potatoes, thinly sliced
Minced fresh parsley
Salt and pepper to taste

In a skillet, melt butter over medium heat. Saute squash and potatoes until tender. Sprinkle with parsley, salt and pepper to taste. **Yield:** 4 servings.

STRAWBERRIES ROMANOFF

- 1 quart fresh strawberries, hulled
- 1/2 cup confectioners' sugar
- 1 cup whipping cream
- 1/4 cup orange juice

Sprinkle strawberries with sugar. Cover and refrigerate 15-20 minutes. Just before serving, whip cream until stiff. Gently stir in orange juice. Fold in berries, or serve individually in bowls topped with the flavored cream. **Yield:** 4-6 servings.

MARIE'S CHICKEN BAKE

Marie Lully, Boulder, Colorado

(PICTURED ON PAGE 42)

1 broiler/fryer chicken (2-1/2 to
  3 pounds), cut up
4 tablespoons butter *or*
  margarine, melted
1/2 cup grated Parmesan cheese
1/2 cup dry bread crumbs
1 teaspoon paprika
1/2 teaspoon dried thyme
2 tablespoons sesame seeds

Dip chicken pieces in butter. Combine remaining ingredients; dip chicken into this crumb mixture. Place on a greased 15-in. x 10-in. x 1-in. baking ban. Drizzle any remaining butter over chicken. Bake at 375° for 45-55 minutes or until chicken is done. **Yield:** 4-6 servings.

PENNSYLVANIA DUTCH COLESLAW

Deb Darr, Falls City, Oregon

(PICTURED ON PAGE 42)

1 medium head green cabbage,
  shredded (about 8 cups)
1 cup shredded red cabbage
4 to 5 carrots, shredded
1 cup mayonnaise
2 tablespoons cider vinegar
1/2 cup sugar
1 teaspoon salt
1/4 teaspoon pepper

In a large bowl, combine cabbage and carrots; set aside. In a small bowl, combine all remaining ingredients; pour over cabbage mixture. Toss well and refrigerate overnight. **Yield:** 12-16 servings.

HOT MILK CAKE

Suzanne Coleman, Rabun Gap, Georgia

(PICTURED ON PAGE 42)

1/2 cup milk
3/4 cup all-purpose flour
1 teaspoon baking powder
1/4 teaspoon salt
3 eggs, room temperature
1 cup sugar
1 teaspoon vanilla extract
TOPPING:
1/3 cup packed brown sugar
1/2 cup chopped pecans
2 tablespoons butter *or*
  margarine, softened
2 tablespoons milk
1 cup shredded coconut

Scald milk; set aside. Combine flour, baking powder and salt; set aside. In a mixing bowl, beat eggs until thick and lemon-colored. Gradually add sugar, blending well. On low speed, alternately mix in milk, dry ingredients and vanilla. Pour batter into a greased 10-in. cast-iron skillet. Bake at 350° for 25-30 minutes or until the cake springs back when lightly touched. Remove cake and preheat broiler. Combine all topping ingredients and sprinkle over cake. Broil 5 inches from the heat until topping bubbles and turns golden brown. Serve warm. **Yield:** 8 servings.

SQUASH-STUFFED CHICKEN

Bernadette Romano, Shaftsbury, Vermont

(PICTURED ON PAGE 45)

3 tablespoons butter *or*
  margarine
1/2 small onion, chopped
1 tablespoon chopped fresh
  parsley
1/2 teaspoon dried basil
2 medium zucchini, shredded
  (about 2-1/2 cups)
3 slices white bread, torn into
  coarse crumbs
1 egg, beaten
3/4 cup shredded Swiss cheese
1/2 teaspoon salt
1/8 teaspoon pepper
4 chicken breast halves (with
  bones and skin)

In a skillet, melt butter over medium-high heat. Saute onion, parsley and basil until the onion is tender. Add zucchini and continue to cook for 2 minutes. Remove from the heat; stir in bread crumbs, egg, cheese, salt and pepper. Carefully loosen the skin of the chicken on one side to form a pocket. Stuff each breast with the zucchini mixture. Bake at 375° for 50-60 minutes or until chicken is done. **Yield:** 4 servings.

CHEDDAR/SQUASH CLOVERLEAF ROLLS

DeDe Waldmann, Monona, Wisconsin

(PICTURED ON PAGE 45)

2 tablespoons sugar
1/4 cup warm water (110°-115°)
1 package (1/4 ounce) active
  dry yeast
1 cup warm milk (110°-115°)
4 tablespoons butter *or*
  margarine, melted, *divided*
1 teaspoon salt
1 cup mashed cooked winter
  squash
3/4 cup shredded cheddar cheese
4 to 4-1/2 cups all-purpose flour
Sesame seeds, optional

In a large mixing bowl, dissolve sugar in water. Sprinkle the yeast over the water and stir gently. Let stand until light and foamy. Stir in milk, 3 tablespoons butter, salt, squash and cheese. Add enough flour to form a soft dough. Turn out onto a lightly floured surface; knead until the dough is no longer sticky, about 5 minutes. Form into a ball and place in a greased bowl, turning once to grease top. Cover and let rise in a warm place until doubled, about 1 hour. Meanwhile, lightly grease 24 muffin cups. Punch down dough. Break off small portions and roll into 1-in. balls. Put three balls into each cup. Cover and let rise in a warm place until doubled, about 30 minutes. Brush tops of rolls with remaining butter; sprinkle with sesame seeds if desired. Bake at 375° for 16-18 minutes or until golden. Serve warm. **Yield:** 2 dozen.

BUTTERNUT APPLE CRISP

Michele Van Dewerker, Roseboom, New York

(PICTURED ON PAGE 45)

3/4 cup packed brown sugar,
  divided
2 tablespoons lemon juice
1 teaspoon ground cinnamon
1/2 teaspoon salt
3 to 4 cups peeled sliced
  uncooked butternut squash
  (about 1-1/2 pounds)
1 can (20 ounces) apple pie
  filling
1/2 cup all-purpose flour
1/2 cup quick-cooking oats
6 tablespoons butter *or*
  margarine, softened

Combine 1/2 cup brown sugar, lemon juice, cinnamon, salt, squash and pie filling. Spoon into 10-in. x 6-in. x 2-in. greased baking dish. Cover and bake at 375° for 30 minutes. Combine remaining ingredients until crumbly. Sprinkle over squash mixture. Bake, uncovered, about 45 minutes longer or until squash is tender. Serve warm. **Yield:** 8 servings.

> **SQUASH SUB:** Winter squash can be substituted for pumpkin in most pie, bread and cookie recipes. Hubbard and banana squash work especially well.

49

MARINATED ZUCCHINI SALAD

Billie Blanton, Kingsport, Tennessee

(PICTURED ON PAGE 45)

6 small zucchini (about 1-1/4 pounds), thinly sliced
1/2 cup chopped green pepper
1/2 cup diced celery
1/2 cup diced onion
1 jar (2 ounces) diced pimiento, drained
2/3 cup vinegar
1/3 cup vegetable oil
1/2 cup sugar
3 tablespoons white wine vinegar
1/2 teaspoon salt
1/2 teaspoon pepper

Combine zucchini, green pepper, celery, onion and pimiento in a medium bowl; set aside. Combine remaining ingredients in a jar; cover tightly and shake vigorously. Pour marinade over vegetables; toss gently. Cover and chill 8 hours or overnight. Serve with a slotted spoon. **Yield:** 8 servings.

ZUCCHINI/HERB PATE

Melissa Sullivan, Iuka, Kansas

(PICTURED ON PAGE 46)

 This tasty dish uses less sugar, salt and fat. Recipe includes *Diabetic Exchanges.*

4 medium zucchini (about 1 pound)
2 teaspoons tarragon vinegar
2 teaspoons sugar
2 teaspoons salt, *divided*
1/2 cup packed fresh parsley sprigs
1/2 cup snipped fresh chives *or* 1/4 cup dried chives
1 package (8 ounces) cream cheese, softened
1/2 teaspoon pepper
Crackers

Line a mixing bowl with a double thickness of cheesecloth. Coarsely shred zucchini into prepared bowl. Sprinkle with vinegar, sugar and 1 teaspoon salt. Toss gently; cover with a towel and set aside for 1 hour. Meanwhile, in a food processor with the chopping blade, mince parsley and chives. Gather ends of cheesecloth, squeezing out as much liquid as possible. Add drained zucchini to food processor and process until pureed. Add cream cheese, pepper and remaining salt; process until smooth. Press pate into a small bowl. Cover and refrigerate overnight. Serve with crackers. **Yield:** 1-1/2 cups. **Diabetic**

Exchanges: One serving (1 tablespoon) equals 1/2 vegetable, 1/2 fat; also, 29 calories, 280 mg sodium, 5 mg cholesterol, 3 gm carbohydrate, 2 gm protein, 2 gm fat.

CONFETTI ZUCCHINI RELISH

Dodie Strobel, Grants Pass, Oregon

(PICTURED ON PAGE 46)

10 cups chopped zucchini
4 cups chopped onion
5 tablespoons salt
1 sweet red pepper, chopped
1 green pepper, chopped
3 cups sugar
2 tablespoons cornstarch
3 teaspoons turmeric
2 teaspoons dry mustard
2 teaspoons celery seed
1/2 teaspoon pepper
2-1/2 cups cider vinegar

Combine zucchini, onion and salt; let stand overnight. Rinse and drain well. Place in a large kettle or Dutch oven along with remaining ingredients; cook until mixture thickens, stirring constantly. Do not overcook. Pack hot into hot sterilized jars, leaving 1/4-in. headspace. Adjust caps. Process 10 minutes in a boiling-water bath. **Yield:** 16 half-pints.

SPAGHETTI SQUASH CASSEROLE

Glenafa Vrchota, Mason City, Iowa

(PICTURED ON PAGE 46)

1 medium spaghetti squash (about 8 inches)
1 cup water
1 tablespoon butter *or* margarine
1 cup chopped onion
2 garlic cloves, minced
1/2 pound fresh mushrooms, sliced
1 teaspoon dried basil
1/2 teaspoon dried oregano
1/4 teaspoon dried thyme
1/2 teaspoon salt
1/4 teaspoon pepper
2 fresh tomatoes, diced
1 cup (8 ounces) ricotta *or* cottage cheese
1 cup (4 ounces) shredded mozzarella cheese
1/4 cup finely chopped parsley
1 cup dry bread crumbs
1/4 cup grated Parmesan cheese

Slice the squash in half lengthwise and scoop out the seeds. Place squash, cut side down, in a baking dish. Add water and cover tightly with foil. Bake at 375° for 20-30 minutes or until easily pierced with a fork. Meanwhile, melt butter in skillet. Add the onion, garlic, mushrooms, herbs and seasonings; saute until onion is transparent. Add the tomatoes; cook until most of the liquid has evaporated. Set aside. Scoop out the squash, separating strands with a fork. Combine squash, tomato mixture and all remaining ingredients except Parmesan cheese. Pour into a greased 2-qt. casserole. Sprinkle with Parmesan cheese. Bake, uncovered, at 375° for 40 minutes or until heated through and top is golden brown. **Yield:** 6 servings.

ZUCCHINI FRITTERS

Mary Dixson, Catlin, Illinois

(PICTURED ON PAGE 47)

Vegetable oil
1/2 cup milk
1 egg, lightly beaten
1 cup all-purpose flour
1-1/2 teaspoons baking powder
1/2 of 1-ounce package ranch-style dip mix
2 cups (8 ounces) shredded zucchini

Fill a deep-fat fryer or skillet with oil to a 2-in. depth. Heat to 375°. Meanwhile, combine milk and egg in a mixing bowl. Stir together dry ingredients and add to egg mixture; blend well. Fold in zucchini. Drop batter by rounded teaspoonful into hot oil. Fry until deep golden brown, turning once. Drain thoroughly on paper towels. **Yield:** 1-1/2 to 2 dozen.

SQUASH CUSTARD PIE

Mary Kelly, Hopland, California

(PICTURED ON PAGE 47)

1 cup mashed cooked winter squash
1 cup whipping *or* heavy cream
1 cup sugar
3 eggs, lightly beaten
1 teaspoon ground ginger
1 teaspoon ground cinnamon
1/2 teaspoon ground nutmeg
Dash salt
1 unbaked pie pastry (9 inches)
Whipped cream *or* topping for garnish

In a mixing bowl, combine all ingredients except for the pie pastry and additional whipped cream. Pour into the pastry; bake at 375° for 10 minutes. Reduce heat to 350°; bake for 45 minutes or until set. Cool on a wire rack. Chill. Serve with a dollop of whipped cream. **Yield:** 8 servings.

DISH TO PASS

Great-tasting dishes to take to any group gathering

CHEESY CHILI CASSEROLE

Phyllis Bidwell, Las Vegas, Nevada

- 2 cups (8 ounces) shredded Monterey Jack cheese
- 2 cups (8 ounces) shredded cheddar cheese
- 2 cans (4 ounces *each*) whole green chilies, rinsed and seeded
- 2 eggs
- 2 tablespoons all-purpose flour
- 1 can (12 ounces) evaporated milk
- 1 can (8 ounces) tomato sauce *or* 1 cup salsa, *divided*

Combine cheeses. In a 10-in. x 6-in. x 2-in. baking dish, layer cheese and chilies. Combine eggs, flour and milk; pour over cheese mixture. Bake at 350° for 30 minutes. Top casserole with half the tomato sauce or salsa; bake 10 minutes longer. Let stand 5 minutes before serving. Pass remaining sauce. **Yield:** 8 servings.

STEAK AND ONION PIE

Dorothea Coe, Port Angeles, Washington

- 1/4 cup all-purpose flour
- 2 teaspoons salt
- 1/2 teaspoon pepper
- 1/2 teaspoon paprika
- Dash ground ginger
- Dash ground allspice
- 1 pound round steak, cut into cubes
- 2 tablespoons cooking oil
- 1 cup sliced onions
- 2 cups diced peeled potatoes
- 2 cups water

PASTRY:
- 1 cup all-purpose flour
- 1/2 teaspoon salt

- 1/3 cup shortening
- 3 tablespoons cold water
- 1 egg, beaten

Combine flour, salt, pepper, paprika, ginger and allspice. Coat meat cubes; reserve remaining flour mixture. In a skillet, heat oil over medium-high burner. Brown meat on all sides. Add onions; cook until tender. Stir in reserved flour mixture. Add potatoes and water; bring to a boil. Reduce heat and simmer 20 minutes or until potatoes are almost tender. Meanwhile, for pastry, combine flour and salt. Cut in shortening. Add water and carefully shape into a ball. Roll out crust to fit a 10-in. pie plate. Spoon meat filling into the pie plate and top with crust. Seal and flute edges. Brush crust with egg. Bake at 450° for 20-25 minutes or until golden. Serve immediately. **Yield:** 6 servings.

GERMAN POTATO SALAD

Mae Wagner, Pickerington, Ohio

- 1-1/2 to 2 pounds bacon
- 3-1/2 pounds potatoes, boiled, peeled and diced (about 7 cups)
- 1-1/2 cups chopped onion
- 1/4 cup all-purpose flour
- 1/4 cup sugar
- 1-1/2 cups water
- 1/4 cup cider vinegar
- 1-1/2 teaspoons salt
- 1/4 teaspoon pepper
- 1/2 cup light cream

In a large skillet, cook the bacon until crisp. Drain, reserving 3 tablespoons drippings. Crumble bacon. In a large bowl, toss bacon with potatoes and onion; set aside. In the drippings, combine flour and sugar. Combine water, vinegar, salt and pepper; stir into skillet. Cook and stir until thickened and bubbly. Stir in cream. Pour over potato mixture; toss gently to coat. Serve warm. **Yield:** 12 servings.

HEAVENLY ONION CASSEROLE

Maryln Rose, Naples, Florida

- 2 tablespoons butter *or* margarine
- 3 medium sweet Spanish onions, sliced
- 8 ounces fresh mushrooms, sliced
- 1 cup (4 ounces) shredded Swiss cheese
- 1 can (10-3/4 ounces)

condensed cream of mushroom soup, undiluted
- 1 can (5 ounces) evaporated milk
- 2 teaspoons soy sauce
- 6 to 8 slices French bread (1/2 inch thick)
- 6 to 8 thin slices Swiss cheese (about 4 ounces)

In a large skillet, melt butter over medium-high heat. Saute onions and mushrooms until tender. Place in a 12-in. x 7-1/2-in. x 2-in. baking dish or 2-qt. casserole. Sprinkle shredded cheese on top. Combine soup, milk and soy sauce; pour over cheese. Top with bread slices and cheese slices. Cover and refrigerate 4 hours or overnight. Bake, loosely covered, at 375° for 30 minutes. Uncover and bake 15-20 minutes longer or until heated through. Let stand 5 minutes before serving. **Yield:** 6-8 servings.

BLOCK PARTY BEANS

LaDonna Daley, Elyria, Ohio

- 2 pounds ground beef
- 2 cups chopped onion
- 1 cup chopped celery
- 1 can (10-3/4 ounces) cream of tomato soup, undiluted
- 1 can (6 ounces) tomato paste
- 1/2 cup ketchup
- 1 can (16 ounces) green beans, drained
- 1 can (17 ounces) lima beans, drained
- 1 can (15-1/2 ounces) wax beans, drained
- 1 can (15 to 16 ounces) chili beans, undrained
- 1 can (16 ounces) pork and beans, undrained
- 1/2 cup packed brown sugar
- 2 tablespoons prepared mustard

In a large Dutch oven, brown beef over medium-high heat. Drain fat. Add onion and celery; cook until tender. Stir in soup, tomato paste and ketchup; simmer 15-20 minutes. Spoon into a large kettle or roaster. Add all remaining ingredients; stir well. Bake, uncovered, at 350° for 1 hour. **Yield:** about 25 servings.

SWEET SECRET: To keep brown sugar from caking up after you open the box, put a piece of lettuce in with it. Change the lettuce whenever it dries out.

WINTER SQUASH SQUARES

Shirley Murphy, Jacksonville, Illinois

(PICTURED ON PAGE 47)

2 cups all-purpose flour
2 cups sugar
2 teaspoons baking powder
1 teaspoon baking soda
1/2 teaspoon ground cinnamon
1/8 teaspoon salt
4 eggs, beaten
2 cups mashed cooked winter squash
1 cup vegetable oil

CREAM CHEESE FROSTING:
1 package (3 ounces) cream cheese, softened
2 cups confectioners' sugar
1 teaspoon vanilla extract
6 tablespoons butter *or* margarine, softened
1 tablespoon milk

In a mixing bowl, combine flour, sugar, baking powder, baking soda, cinnamon and salt. Stir in eggs, squash and oil; mix well. Spread into a greased 15-in. x 10-in. x 1-in. baking pan. Bake at 350° for 25 to 30 minutes or until bars test done. Cool on a wire rack. Meanwhile, for frosting, beat together cream cheese, confectioners' sugar, vanilla and butter. Add milk; stir until smooth. Frost cooled cake. Cut into squares. **Yield:** 4 dozen.

GARDEN HARVEST CHILI

Judy Sloter, Charles City, Iowa

(PICTURED ON PAGE 46)

 This tasty dish uses less sugar, salt and fat. Recipe includes *Diabetic Exchanges*.

2 tablespoons cooking oil
2 garlic cloves, minced
1 medium green pepper, chopped
1 medium sweet red pepper, chopped
1-1/2 cups sliced fresh mushrooms
1/2 cup chopped onion
1 can (28 ounces) whole tomatoes, cut up, undrained
1 can (15 ounces) tomato sauce
2 tablespoons chili powder
2 teaspoons sugar
1 teaspoon ground cumin
1 can (16 ounces) kidney beans, rinsed and drained
2 cups sliced zucchini
1 package (10 ounces) frozen sweet corn, defrosted
1-1/2 cups (6 ounces) shredded cheddar cheese, optional

In a skillet, heat oil over medium-high. Saute garlic, peppers, mushrooms and onion until tender. Add tomatoes with liquid, tomato sauce, chili powder, sugar and cumin; heat to boiling. Reduce heat to low; add beans, zucchini and corn. Simmer, uncovered, about 10 minutes or until zucchini is tender. Spoon into bowls; sprinkle with cheese if desired. **Yield:** 6 servings (2-1/2 quarts). **Diabetic Exchanges:** One serving (prepared with low-salt tomato sauce and no cheese) equals 2 starch, 2 vegetable, 1 fat; also, 252 calories, 675 mg sodium, 0 mg cholesterol, 44 gm carbohydrate, 10 gm protein, 7 gm fat.

SQUASH AND BROCCOLI STIR-FRY

Erlene Cornelius, Spring City, Tennessee

(PICTURED ON PAGE 46)

 This tasty dish uses less sugar, salt and fat. Recipe includes *Diabetic Exchanges*.

1 tablespoon lemon juice
2 teaspoons honey
2 tablespoons cooking oil
1 pound butternut squash, peeled, seeded and cut into 1/4-inch slices
1 garlic clove, minced
1/4 teaspoon ground ginger
1 cup fresh broccoli florets
1/2 cup bias-sliced celery
1/2 cup thinly sliced onion
2 tablespoons sunflower seeds

Combine lemon juice and honey; set aside. In a wok or large skillet, heat oil on medium-high. Add squash, garlic and ginger. Stir-fry about 3 minutes. Add the broccoli, celery and onion; stir-fry 3-4 minutes or until crisp-tender. Remove from heat and quickly toss with the honey mixture. Sprinkle with sunflower seeds. Serve immediately. **Yield:** 6 servings. **Diabetic Exchanges:** One serving equals 2 vegetable, 1-1/2 fat; also, 113 calories, 20 mg sodium, 0 mg cholesterol, 13 gm carbohydrate, 2 gm protein, 7 gm fat.

HERB BREAD

Darlene Miller, Linn, Missouri

 This tasty dish uses less sugar, salt and fat. Recipe includes *Diabetic Exchanges*.

3 cups whole wheat flour
5 to 5-1/2 cups all-purpose flour, *divided*
2 packages (1/4 ounce *each*) active dry yeast

3 tablespoons sugar
1 tablespoon salt
1 teaspoon dried sage
1/2 teaspoon dried thyme
1/2 teaspoon dried marjoram
1 small onion, minced
3 tablespoons cooking oil
3 cups warm water (120°-130°)
Milk
2 tablespoons grated Parmesan cheese

In a large mixing bowl, combine whole wheat flour, 1 cup all-purpose flour, yeast, sugar, salt, herbs, onion, oil and water. Beat with an electric mixer on low until moistened, then beat for 3 minutes at medium. By hand, stir in enough of the remaining flour to form a stiff dough. Place in a greased bowl, turning once to grease top. Cover and allow to rise until doubled, about 1 hour. Punch dough down. Shape into two balls and place in two greased 2-qt. casseroles. Cover and let rise until almost doubled, about 45 minutes. Brush tops with milk and sprinkle with Parmesan cheese. Bake at 350° for 40-45 minutes. Remove from casseroles to cool on a wire rack. **Yield:** 2 loaves (40 slices). **Diabetic Exchanges:** One serving (one slice) equals 1-1/4 starch; also, 99 calories, 63 mg sodium, trace cholesterol, 21 gm carbohydrate, 3 gm protein, trace fat.

NORWEGIAN MEATBALLS

Jeane Jenson, Stillwater, Minnesota

2 eggs, beaten
1 cup milk
1 cup dry bread crumbs
1/2 cup minced onion
2 teaspoons salt
2 teaspoons sugar
1/2 teaspoon ground ginger
1/2 teaspoon ground nutmeg
1/2 teaspoon ground allspice
1/4 teaspoon pepper
2 pounds lean ground beef
1 pound ground pork

GRAVY:
3 tablespoons butter *or* margarine
2 tablespoons minced onion
5 tablespoons all-purpose flour
4 cups beef broth
1/2 cup heavy cream
Dash cayenne pepper
Dash white pepper

In a mixing bowl, combine eggs, milk, bread crumbs, onion and seasonings. Let stand until crumbs absorb milk. Add meat; stir until well blended. Shape into 1-in. meatballs. Place on a greased jelly roll pan. Bake at 400° until browned, about 18 minutes. Set aside. For gravy, melt butter over medium-high heat in a large skillet. Saute onion until tender. Stir in flour and brown lightly. Slowly add broth; cook and stir until smooth and thickened. Blend in cream, cayenne pepper and white pepper. Gently stir in meatballs; heat through but do not boil. **Yield:** about 16 servings.

CHERRY/ALMOND QUICK BREAD

Nancy Reichert, Thomasville, Georgia

1 cup sugar
1/2 cup butter *or* margarine, softened
2 eggs
1 teaspoon almond extract
2 cups all-purpose flour
1 teaspoon baking soda
1/2 teaspoon salt
1 cup buttermilk
1 cup chopped almonds
1 jar (6 ounces) maraschino cherries, drained and chopped

In a large mixing bowl, cream sugar and butter. Add eggs, one at a time, beating well after each addition. Blend in extract. Combine dry ingredients; blend into creamed mixture alternately with the buttermilk. Stir in the almonds and cherries. Pour into a greased and floured 9-in. x 5-in. x 3-in. loaf pan. Bake at 350° for about 70 minutes or until loaf tests done. Remove from pan and cool on a wire rack. **Yield:** 1 loaf.

ORANGE BOWKNOTS

Pam Hansen Taylor, Houston, Texas

1 cup milk
1/2 cup shortening
1/3 cup sugar
1 teaspoon salt
1 package (1/4 ounce) active dry yeast
1/4 cup warm water (110°-115°)
2 eggs, beaten
1/4 cup orange juice
Grated peel of 2 oranges
5 to 6 cups all-purpose flour, *divided*
ORANGE GLAZE:
2 tablespoons orange juice
2 teaspoons grated orange peel
1 cup confectioners' sugar

In a saucepan, heat milk, shortening, sugar and salt. Cool to lukewarm. Dissolve yeast in water. In a large mixing bowl, combine yeast with milk mixture, eggs, juice, peel and 3 cups flour. Mix until smooth. Stir in enough remaining

flour to form a soft dough. Knead until smooth and elastic, about 6-8 minutes. Place dough in a greased bowl; cover and let rise in a warm place until doubled, about 1-1/2 hours. Punch dough down; let rest 15 minutes. Roll dough into a 16-in. x 10-in. rectangle. Cut into 16 1-in. strips. Tie strips into knots; place on greased baking sheets. Cover and let rise until doubled, about 1 hour. Bake at 400° for about 10 minutes or until golden brown. Cool on wire rack. Combine all glaze ingredients; spread over rolls. **Yield:** 16 rolls.

APPLES 'N' CREAM PANCAKE

Ruth Schafer, Defiance, Ohio

1/2 cup milk
2 eggs
1/2 cup all-purpose flour
1/4 teaspoon salt
1 to 2 tablespoons butter *or* margarine
1/4 cup packed brown sugar
1 package (3 ounces) cream cheese, softened
1/2 cup sour cream
1/2 teaspoon vanilla extract
1-1/2 cups thinly sliced unpeeled apples
1/4 cup chopped walnuts

In a small mixing bowl, combine milk, eggs, flour and salt. Beat until smooth. Heat a cast-iron or ovenproof skillet in a 450° oven until hot. Add butter to the skillet; spread over entire bottom. Pour in batter; bake for 10 minutes or until golden brown. Meanwhile, combine sugar and cream cheese. Blend in sour cream and vanilla. Fill pancake with 3/4 cup cream cheese mixture and top with apples. Spread remaining cream cheese mixture over apples and sprinkle with nuts. Cut into wedges and serve immediately. **Yield:** 4-6 servings.

BRUNCH EGG CASSEROLE

Lelia Brown, Annandale, Virginia

2 cups unseasoned croutons
1 cup (4 ounces) shredded cheddar cheese
4 eggs, beaten
2 cups milk
1/2 teaspoon salt
1/2 teaspoon dry mustard
1/8 teaspoon onion powder
Dash pepper
4 slices bacon, fried, drained and crumbled

Place croutons and cheese in the bottom of a greased 10-in. x 6-in. x 1-3/4-in. baking dish. Combine eggs, milk and seasonings; pour into baking dish. Sprinkle with bacon. Bake at 325° for 1 hour or until set. Serve immediately. **Yield:** 6 servings.

CHICKEN NOODLE SOUP

Diane Edgecomb, Humboldt, South Dakota

1 stewing chicken (2 to 3 pounds)
2-1/2 quarts water
3 teaspoons salt
2 chicken bouillon cubes
1/2 medium onion, chopped
1/8 teaspoon pepper
1/4 teapoon dried marjoram
1/4 teaspoon dried thyme
1 bay leaf
1 cup diced carrots
1 cup diced celery
1-1/2 cups uncooked fine noodles

In a large soup kettle, place chicken and all ingredients except noodles. Cover and bring to a boil; skim broth. Reduce heat; cover and simmer 1-1/2 hours or until chicken is tender. Remove chicken from broth; allow to cool. Debone chicken and cut into chunks. Skim fat from broth; bring to a boil. Add noodles; cook until noodles are done. Return chicken to kettle; adjust seasonings to taste. Remove bay leaf before serving. **Yield:** 8-10 servings.

CITRUS-TOPPED PORK CHOPS

Brenda Wood, Egbert, Ontario

1 tablespoon cooking oil
6 loin pork chops (1 inch thick)
Salt and pepper to taste
1/4 teaspoon paprika
1/2 cup apple jelly
1 cup orange juice
1/2 teaspoon lemon juice
1 teaspoon dry mustard
Dash ground ginger
6 orange slices
6 lemon slices

In a large skillet, heat oil over medium-high. Brown chops on both sides. Season with salt, pepper and paprika. Combine jelly, juices, mustard and ginger. Pour over chops. Simmer, covered, for 15 minutes. Turn chops; cover and simmer 15 minutes. Top each chop with an orange and lemon slice. Cover and cook 6-8 minutes longer or until chops are done. **Yield:** 6 servings.

GLAZED PEACH PIE

Trudy Dunn, Dallas, Texas

- 1 cup sugar
- 1/4 cup cornstarch
- Dash salt
- Dash ground nutmeg
- 2 tablespoons water
- 1 tablespoon lemon juice
- 2-1/2 cups pureed peeled fresh peaches
- 3-1/2 cups sliced peeled fresh peaches
- 1 pie pastry (9 inches), baked

In a saucepan, combine sugar, cornstarch, salt and nutmeg. Stir in water, lemon juice and pureed peaches. Cook over medium heat, stirring constantly, about 5 minutes or until mixture is thickened. Pour all but 1/2 cup of glaze into the pie shell. Top with sliced peaches and brush with reserved glaze. Chill for at least 3 hours. **Yield:** 8 servings.

BROCCOLI DELIGHT SALAD

Anita Jordan, Sedalia, Missouri

- 5 cups chopped fresh broccoli
- 1/2 cup raisins
- 1/4 cup chopped red onion
- 2 tablespoons sugar
- 3 tablespoons vinegar
- 1 cup mayonnaise
- 10 bacon slices, cooked and crumbled
- 1 cup sunflower seeds

In a large salad bowl, combine broccoli, raisins and onion. In a small bowl, combine sugar, vinegar and mayonnaise. Pour over broccoli; toss to coat. Refrigerate. Just before serving, sprinkle with bacon and sunflower seeds; toss. **Yield:** 6-8 servings.

BARBECUED RIBS

Frances Campbell, Charlotte, North Carolina

- 3 to 3-1/2 pounds pork spareribs
- 2 tablespoons cooking oil
- 1 medium onion, chopped
- 1 cup ketchup
- 1 cup hot water
- 2 tablespoons vinegar
- 1 tablespoon Worcestershire sauce
- 1 teaspoon dry mustard
- 1/2 teaspoon salt
- 1 tablespoon brown sugar
- 1/4 teaspoon cayenne pepper

1/4 teaspoon pepper

Place ribs on a jelly roll pan. Cover tightly with foil; bake at 450° for 45 minutes or until tender. Drain off any fat. In a saucepan, combine all remaining ingredients and bring to a boil. Pour over ribs. Reduce heat to 350°; bake, uncovered, for 1 hour, basting frequently. **Yield:** 6 servings.

ZUCCHINI/POTATO SOUP

Christine Gibson, Fontana, Wisconsin

- 5 cups chicken broth
- 4 small zucchini (about 1 pound), thinly sliced
- 1 large potato, peeled, halved and thinly sliced
- 1 large onion, thinly sliced
- 3 eggs
- 2 tablespoons lemon juice
- 2 teaspoons dried dill weed

Salt and pepper to taste

In a saucepan, bring broth to a boil. Stir in zucchini, potato and onion. Reduce heat and simmer, covered, 15 minutes or until vegetables are tender. In a small bowl, beat eggs; blend in lemon juice and 1/2 cup hot broth. Stir back into the saucepan. Heat over medium for 1 minute, stirring constantly. Do not boil. Stir in dill; season with salt and pepper. Serve immediately. **Yield:** about 2 quarts.

STUFFED CABBAGE ROLLS

Jean Parsons, Sarver, Pennsylvania

- 1 large head cabbage
- 1 cup quick-cooking rice, cooked and cooled
- 1 pound lean ground beef
- 1 medium onion, chopped
- 2 tablespoons Worcestershire sauce
- 1/2 teaspoon salt
- 1/4 teaspoon pepper
- 1 can (10-3/4 ounces) condensed cream of tomato soup, undiluted, *divided*
- 1/2 cup water

Cook cabbage in boiling water only until leaves fall off head. Reserve 14-16 large leaves for rolls and set remaining cabbage aside. Combine rice, beef, onion, Worcestershire sauce, salt, pepper and 1/4 cup soup; mix well. Put 2 to 3 tablespoons meat mixture on each cabbage leaf. Fold in sides, starting at an unfolded edge, and roll up leaf completely to enclose meat. Repeat with remaining meat and leaves. Line a Dutch oven with leftover cab-

bage. Combine remaining soup and water; pour over cabbage. Stack cabbage rolls on top of sauce. Cover. Bring to a boil; reduce heat and simmer on low for 1 to 1-1/2 hours or until rolls are tender. Remove rolls and cabbage. If desired, sauce may be thickened by boiling over high heat. Spoon sauce over rolls and cabbage and serve immediately. **Yield:** 4-6 servings.

PICNIC PEAS

Joyce Sander, Evansville, Indiana

- 1 tablespoon cooking oil
- 1 cup chopped green pepper
- 1 cup chopped onion
- 1 cup minced celery
- 1 tablespoon sugar
- 1 bay leaf
- 1 can (15 ounces) black-eyed peas, rinsed and drained
- 1 can (14-1/2 ounces) tomatoes, chopped, liquid reserved
- 1/2 teaspoon salt
- 1/4 teaspoon pepper
- 4 bacon slices, cooked and crumbled

In a skillet, heat oil over medium-high. Saute green pepper, onion and celery. Add sugar, bay leaf, peas, tomatoes, half the tomato liquid, salt and pepper. Reduce heat and simmer 15 minutes. Remove to a bowl and sprinkle with bacon. Serve hot or at room temperature. **Yield:** 6 servings.

CRAB SALAD SUPREME

Mrs. A. Mayer, Richmond, Virginia

- 2 cups crabmeat
- 1/2 cup minced green onions
- 1/2 cup diced celery
- 1/2 cup minced green pepper
- 1 tablespoon dry mustard
- 1 teaspoon salt
- 1/4 teaspoon pepper
- 2 teaspoons celery seed
- Shredded lettuce
- 4 hard-cooked eggs, sliced
- 4 tomatoes, cut into wedges

SAUCE:
- 1/3 cup mayonnaise
- 1/3 cup sour cream
- 1/3 cup chili sauce
- 2 teaspoons lemon juice

Combine first eight ingredients. Combine sauce ingredients; pour over salad and toss. Spoon onto lettuce on individual plates or a serving platter; garnish with eggs and tomatoes. Refrigerate until serving. **Yield:** 4-6 servings.

S avor the fresh fruits of the summer (remember to freeze fruits for winter cooking, too) by preparing the recipes shown above. They're perfect treats to serve at your next celebration.

Start your day with a piping hot Blueberry Cream Muffin or a hearty slice of Peachy Sour Cream Coffee Cake. Family picnics will be memorable when you serve the Ozark Mountain Berry Pie with lots of creamy hand-cranked ice cream. And don't forget to pass the Lemon Filbert Tea Bars—they're perfect on a summer day!

FRUITY FAVORITES. Clockwise from top left: **Blueberry Cream Muffins, Ozark Mountain Berry Pie, Lemon Filbert Tea Bars, Peachy Sour Cream Coffee Cake** (all recipes on page 57).

Who could resist a slice of this wonderfully moist cake spread with a scrumptious cream cheese frosting? A perfect dessert choice for Mother's Day, a birthday or any special occasion, this delicious cake will likely take top honors in your household!

GIFT OF LOVE. Zucchini Carrot Cake (page 57).

BLUEBERRY CREAM MUFFINS

Lillian Van der Harst, Center Lovell, Maine

(PICTURED ON PAGE 55)

4 eggs
2 cups sugar
1 cup vegetable oil
1 teaspoon vanilla extract
4 cups all-purpose flour
1 teaspoon salt
1 teaspoon baking soda
2 teaspoons baking powder
2 cups (16 ounces) sour cream
2 cups fresh blueberries

In a mixing bowl, beat eggs. Gradually add sugar. While beating, slowly pour in oil; add vanilla. Combine dry ingredients; add alternately with the sour cream to the egg mixture. Gently fold in blueberries. Spoon into greased muffin tins. Bake at 400° for 20 minutes. **Yield:** 24 muffins.

PEACHY SOUR CREAM COFFEE CAKE

Alice Brandt, Marengo, Illinois

(PICTURED ON PAGE 55)

STREUSEL TOPPING/FILLING:
2 cups chopped pecans
1/3 cup packed brown sugar
3 tablespoons sugar
1 teaspoon ground cinnamon
CAKE:
1/2 cup butter-flavored shortening
1 cup sugar
2 eggs
2 cups all-purpose flour
1-1/2 teaspoons baking powder
1/2 teaspoon baking soda
1/2 teaspoon salt
1 cup (8 ounces) sour cream
1 teaspoon vanilla extract
2 cups sliced peeled fresh peaches

Combine all streusel ingredients; set aside. In a large mixing bowl, cream shortening and sugar until fluffy. Beat in eggs. Combine all dry ingredients; add alternately with the sour cream and vanilla to the creamed mixture. Beat until smooth. Pour half the batter into a 9-in. springform pan. Sprinkle with 1 cup of the streusel. Top with remaining batter and 1/2 cup streusel. Bake at 350° for 30 minutes. Arrange peaches over cake; sprinkle with remaining streusel. Bake an additional 30-40 minutes or until cake tests done. Cool cake 10 minutes before removing

sides of pan. Serve warm or at room temperature. **Yield:** 12 servings.

OZARK MOUNTAIN BERRY PIE

Elaine Moody, Clever, Missouri

(PICTURED ON PAGE 55)

1 cup sugar
Dash salt
1/4 cup cornstarch
1/2 teaspoon ground cinnamon, optional
1 cup blueberries
1 cup strawberries
3/4 cup blackberries
3/4 cup red raspberries
1/2 cup water
2 tablespoons lemon juice
2 tablespoons butter *or* margarine
Pastry for a double-crust pie (9 inches)

In a saucepan, combine sugar, salt, cornstarch, and cinnamon if desired. Stir in berries. Add water and lemon juice. Cook over medium heat just to the boiling point. Pour into pie shell; dot with butter. Top with a lattice or full crust. If using a full crust, cut slits in the top, brush with milk and sprinkle with sugar. Bake at 350° for about 45 minutes or until the crust is golden. **Yield:** 8 servings.

LEMON FILBERT TEA BARS

Cathee Bethel, Philomath, Oregon

(PICTURED ON PAGE 55)

1/2 cup butter *or* margarine
1 cup plus 2 tablespoons all-purpose flour, *divided*
1/4 cup confectioners' sugar
2 eggs
1 cup sugar
1 teaspoon grated lemon peel
2 tablespoons lemon juice
1/2 teaspoon baking powder
1/2 cup ground toasted filberts
Additional confectioners' sugar

In a mixing bowl, combine butter, 1 cup flour and confectioners' sugar. Press into the bottom of an 11-1/2-in. x 7-1/2-in. baking pan. Bake at 350° for 10 minutes. Combine the remaining ingredients except additional confectioners' sugar. Pour over the crust; bake for 20 minutes. Cool. Cut into squares and sprinkle with confectioners' sugar. **Yield:** about 15 bars.

ZUCCHINI CARROT CAKE

Mary Spill, Tierra Amarilla, New Mexico

(PICTURED ON PAGE 56)

4 eggs
2 cups sugar
1-1/3 cups vegetable oil
2-1/2 cups all-purpose flour
2 teaspoons baking soda
2 teaspoons baking powder
2 teaspoons ground cinnamon
1 teaspoon ground cloves
1 teaspoon ground allspice
1 teaspoon ground ginger
1/2 teaspoon ground nutmeg
1 teaspoon salt
2 cups finely shredded carrots
2 cups finely shredded zucchini
1 cup coarsely chopped pecans *or* walnuts
FROSTING:
1 package (8 ounces) cream cheese, softened
1/2 cup butter *or* margarine, softened
5 cups confectioners' sugar
2 teaspoons vanilla extract
Whole *or* chopped pecans *or* walnuts for garnish, optional

In a large mixing bowl, beat eggs and sugar until frothy. Gradually beat in oil. Combine dry ingredients; add to batter. Beat 4 minutes. Stir in carrots, zucchini and nuts. Pour into three greased 9-in. baking pans. Bake at 350° for about 35 minutes or until top springs back when lightly touched. Cool 5 minutes before removing from pans. Cool thoroughly on a wire rack. For frosting, beat cream cheese and butter in a large mixing bowl until smooth. Add sugar and vanilla. Continue beating until sugar is dissolved. Spread between the layers and over the top and sides of the cake. Garnish with whole or chopped nuts if desired. **Yield:** 12-14 servings.

BAKED ASPARAGUS DIP

Sandra Baratka, Phillips, Wisconsin

1 pound diced cooked fresh asparagus, drained
1 cup grated Parmesan cheese
1 cup mayonnaise
Snack rye breads

Blend asparagus, cheese and mayonnaise. Place in a 2-cup ovenproof bowl. Bake at 375° for 20 minutes. Serve with snack rye breads. **Yield:** 6-8 appetizer servings.

CHERRY PINEAPPLE SALAD

Leona Luecking, West Burlington, Iowa

3 packages (3 ounces *each*) cherry-flavored gelatin
2-1/3 cups boiling water
1 can (20 ounces) pineapple tidbits, liquid drained and reserved
2 cans (16-1/2 ounces *each*) pitted dark sweet cherries, liquid drained and reserved
1/3 cup lemon juice
1/3 cup whipping cream
1/3 cup mayonnaise
2 packages (3 ounces *each*) cream cheese, softened
Dash salt
1/2 cup coarsely chopped nuts

In a mixing bowl, dissolve gelatin in water. Combine pineapple and cherry juices to measure 2-1/2 cups; add along with lemon juice to gelatin. Divide gelatin in half. Set half of the gelatin aside and chill other half until partially set. Fold pineapple into chilled gelatin; pour into a 13-in. x 9-in. x 2-in. pan. Chill until almost firm. Whip cream, mayonnaise, cream cheese and salt until light and fluffy. Spread over chilled gelatin layer. Refrigerate until firm. Chill remaining gelatin mixture until partially set. Fold in cherries and nuts; spread over cream cheese layer. Chill for at least 3 hours. **Yield:** 12-16 servings.

CURRIED CHICKEN FRUIT SALAD

Carol Mead, Los Alamos, New Mexico

1 can (11 ounces) mandarin oranges, drained
1 can (8 ounces) pineapple tidbits, drained
1 can (8 ounces) water chestnuts, drained
4 cups cubed cooked chicken
2 cups seedless red *or* green grapes, halved
1 cup chopped celery
Lettuce leaves
Sliced almonds
DRESSING:
1-1/2 cups mayonnaise
1 tablespoon soy sauce
1 tablespoon lemon juice
1-1/2 teaspoons curry powder

In a large bowl, combine the oranges, pineapple, water chestnuts, chicken, grapes and celery. In a small bowl, combine all dressing ingredients. Pour over salad; toss well to coat. Chill 1

hour. Serve on a bed of lettuce; sprinkle with almonds. **Yield:** 8 servings.

STRAWBERRY SPINACH SALAD

Jamie Stoneman
Winston-Salem, North Carolina

2 bunches fresh spinach, washed and dried
1 pint fresh strawberries, hulled and sliced
1/2 cup sugar
2 tablespoons sesame seeds
1 tablespoon poppy seeds
1-1/2 teaspoons finely chopped onion
1/4 teaspoon Worcestershire sauce
1/4 teaspoon paprika
1/2 cup vegetable oil
1/4 cup cider vinegar

Arrange spinach and strawberries on individual salad plates or in a large salad bowl. Place the next six ingredients in a blender or food processor. With unit running, add oil and vinegar in a steady stream. Blend until thickened. Drizzle over salad; serve immediately. **Yield:** 6-8 servings.

BUTTERY BLUEBERRY COBBLER

Marjorie Green, South Haven, Michigan

2 cups fresh *or* frozen blueberries
1 tablespoon lemon juice
1-1/2 cups sugar, *divided*
1/2 cup butter *or* margarine
1 cup all-purpose flour
2 teaspoons baking powder
1/2 teaspoon salt
3/4 cup milk
1 egg, beaten
Whipped cream *or* topping

In a saucepan, combine berries, lemon juice and 1/2 cup sugar. Bring to a boil; remove from the heat. Set aside. Put butter in a 12-in. x 7-in. baking pan;

place in oven until butter melts. In a small mixing bowl, combine remaining sugar with flour, baking powder, salt, milk and egg. Pour over melted butter. *Do not stir.* Spoon reserved berry mixture over batter. *Do not stir.* Bake at 350° for 40-45 minutes or until golden brown. Serve at room temperature with whipped cream or topping. **Yield:** about 10-12 servings.

CHOCOLATE CHIP OATMEAL MUFFINS

Cheryl Bohn, Dominion City, Manitoba

1/2 cup butter *or* margarine
3/4 cup packed brown sugar
1 egg
1 cup all-purpose flour
1 teaspoon baking powder
1/4 teaspoon baking soda
1/4 teaspoon salt
3/4 cup applesauce
1 cup rolled oats
1 cup (6 ounces) semisweet chocolate chips

In a large mixing bowl, cream butter and sugar. Beat in egg. Combine next four ingredients; add alternately with applesauce to the creamed mixture. Stir in oats and chips. Fill greased or paper-lined muffin tins 3/4 full. Bake at 350° for 25 minutes. **Yield:** 12 muffins.

PORK CHOP AND CHILIES CASSEROLE

Mickey O'Neal, Chula Vista, California

1 tablespoon cooking oil
4 rib pork chops (3/4 to 1 inch thick)
1 medium onion, chopped
1 can (4 ounces) chopped green chilies
1/2 cup chopped celery
1-1/2 cups uncooked instant rice
1 can (10-3/4 ounces) cream of mushroom soup, undiluted
1 soup can water
3 tablespoons soy sauce

In a skillet, heat oil over medium-high. Brown pork chops on both sides. Remove and set aside. In the same skillet, saute onion, chilies and celery until onion is tender. Stir in rice; saute until lightly browned. Add soup, water and soy sauce; blend well. Place in a greased 2-qt. casserole. Top with pork chops. Bake at 350° for about 30 minutes or until rice is tender. **Yield:** 4 servings.

ENGLISH PASTIES

Margaret Johnson, Yale, Michigan

PASTRY:
  1-1/2 cups all-purpose flour
  1/4 teaspoon salt
  1/2 cup shortening
  1/4 cup cold water *or* milk
FILLING:
  1/2 pound boneless beef sirloin, cubed
  1/4 pound boneless pork steak, cubed
  2 medium potatoes, peeled and cubed
  1 small onion, chopped
  1/2 teaspoon salt
  1/4 teaspoon pepper
  1 tablespoon butter
  1 egg, beaten, optional
  2 teaspoons water

Combine flour and salt. Cut in shortening. Add enough water or milk to moisten dry ingredients. Shape into a ball. Cover and set aside. For filling, toss together beef, pork, potatoes, onion, salt and pepper. Divide the pastry in half and roll each into a 10-in. circle. Divide the filling over the center of each pastry; dot each with 1/2 tablespoon butter. Fold pastry over the filling, sealing edges tightly. Cut slits in the top of the pasties. If desired, brush tops with egg. Place on a greased baking sheet. Bake at 400° for 45 minutes. Spoon 1 teaspoon water per pasty in slits. Reduce heat to 350°; bake 15 minutes longer or until golden. **Yield:** 4 servings.

CHICKEN ASPARAGUS DIVAN

Donna Stewart, West Chester, Ohio

  4 boneless skinless chicken breast halves
Onion and celery with tops
Water
  1/2 teaspoon salt
  2 tablespoons chopped onion

  1/2 cup grated Parmesan cheese, *divided*
  1 can (10-3/4 ounces) cream of chicken soup, undiluted
  1 pound fresh asparagus spears, cooked until crisp-tender
  1/3 cup whipping cream
  1/3 cup mayonnaise

In a skillet, place chicken, onion, celery, water to cover and salt. Bring to a boil; reduce heat and simmer until chicken is tender. Drain and discard liquid. Combine chopped onion, 1/3 cup Parmesan cheese and soup. Spread half of the mixture in the bottom of a 13-in. x 9-in. x 2-in. baking pan. Top with asparagus, then chicken and remaining soup mixture. Bake at 350°, covered, for 25 minutes or until heated through. Combine cream and mayonnaise. Spread over chicken. Sprinkle remaining Parmesan cheese on top. Brown lightly under broiler. Serve immediately. **Yield:** 4 servings.

CHERRY SWIRL COFFEE CAKE

Charlene Griffin, Minocqua, Wisconsin

  1-1/2 cups sugar
  1/2 cup butter *or* margarine
  1/2 cup shortening
  1/2 teaspoon baking powder
  1 teaspoon vanilla extract
  1 teaspoon almond extract
  4 eggs
  3 cups all-purpose flour
  1 can (21 ounces) cherry pie filling
GLAZE:
  1 cup confectioners' sugar
  1 to 2 tablespoons milk

In a mixing bowl, blend the first seven ingredients on low speed. Increase to high speed and whip for 3 minutes. Stir in flour. Spread 2/3 of the batter over the bottom of a greased 15-1/2-in. x 10-1/2-in. x 1-in. jelly roll pan. Spread pie filling over batter; drop remaining batter by tablespoonsful over all. Bake at 350° for

---

ASPARAGUS TIPS: Fresh asparagus stores longer if kept standing, cut side down, in an inch of water in the refrigerator. Use a tall pitcher or large beverage container and replace water as needed.

● Don't toss out the tough ends of asparagus spears. Save them for soup. Simmer them until tender, then puree in a blender or food processor until smooth.

40 minutes or until golden. Meanwhile, combine glaze ingredients. Drizzle over cake while warm. Cake is best if served immediately. **Yield:** 18-20 servings.

FROZEN ICE CREAM DELIGHT

Sue Bracken, State College, Pennsylvania

  2-1/2 cups cream-filled chocolate cookie crumbs, *divided*
  1/2 cup butter *or* margarine, melted
  1/2 cup sugar
  1/2 gallon chocolate, coffee *or* vanilla ice cream, softened
  1-1/2 cups salted peanuts
  1 carton (8 ounces) frozen whipped topping, thawed
CHOCOLATE SAUCE:
  2 cups confectioners' sugar
  2/3 cup semisweet chocolate chips
  1 can (12 ounces) evaporated milk
  1/2 cup butter *or* margarine
  1 teaspoon vanilla extract

Combine 2 cups cookie crumbs with butter and sugar. Press into the bottom of a 13-in. x 9-in. x 2-in. baking pan. Freeze for 15 minutes. Spread ice cream over crumbs; freeze until firm, about 3 hours. Meanwhile, combine first four sauce ingredients in a saucepan; bring to a boil. Boil for 8 minutes. Remove from the heat and stir in vanilla; allow to cool to room temperature. Spoon sauce over ice cream; sprinkle with nuts. Freeze until firm. Spread whipped topping over nuts and sprinkle with remaining cookie crumbs. Freeze at least 3 hours before serving. Can be stored in the freezer for up to a week. **Yield:** 12-16 servings.

CUCUMBER PARTY SANDWICHES

Rebecca Rose, Mount Washington, Kentucky

  1 package (8 ounces) cream cheese, softened
  1/2 envelope (2 teaspoons) dry Italian salad dressing mix
  2 tablespoons mayonnaise
  30 slices snack rye bread
  30 thin slices cucumber
Fresh dill sprigs

In a bowl, combine the cream cheese, dressing mix and mayonnaise. Allow to stand at least 30 minutes. Spread on rye bread. Top with a slice of cucumber and a sprig of dill. Cover and refrigerate until serving time. **Yield:** 30 appetizers.

PRAIRIE APPLE CRUNCH

Florence Palmer, Paris, Illinois

      6 large baking apples, peeled
        and sliced
      1/2 cup sugar
      1/2 teaspoon ground cinnamon
      1/2 teaspoon ground nutmeg
  Dash salt
      1 cup packed brown sugar
      1 cup all-purpose flour
      1/2 cup butter or margarine,
        melted
  Cream, optional

Place apples in a greased 12-in. x 7-1/2-in. x 2-in. baking dish. Sprinkle with the sugar, cinnamon, nutmeg and salt. Combine brown sugar, flour and butter; sprinkle over apple mixture. Bake at 350° for 40-45 minutes or until apples are tender. Serve warm or at room temperature, with cream if desired. **Yield:** 10-12 servings.

APPLE CAKE WITH BUTTERMILK SAUCE

Donni Way, Plattsburgh, New York

      3 cups all-purpose flour
      1 teaspoon baking soda
      1/2 teaspoon salt
      1 teaspoon ground cinnamon
      3 eggs
      2 cups sugar
  1-1/4 cups vegetable oil
      1 teaspoon vanilla extract
      1/4 cup orange juice
      2 cups chopped unpeeled apples
      1 cup chopped walnuts
      1 cup flaked coconut
  BUTTERMILK SAUCE:
      1 cup sugar
      1/2 cup butter or margarine
      1/2 teaspoon baking soda
      1/2 cup buttermilk

  Whipped cream, optional

Combine flour, baking soda, salt and cinnamon; set aside. In a large mixing bowl, beat eggs. Add sugar, oil, vanilla and orange juice. On low speed, blend in flour mixture. Fold in apples, walnuts

and coconut. Pour into a greased and floured 10-in. tube pan. Bake at 325° for 1-1/4 hours or until the cake tests done. Invert cake onto a large plate or platter. Deeply puncture the top of the warm cake with a skewer or pick. In a small saucepan, bring all sauce ingredients to a boil, stirring frequently. Immediately spoon 1-1/4 cups of sauce slowly over the top of the cake, then pour the remainder down the sides. Cool. Serve with whipped cream if desired. **Yield:** 16 servings.

CHICKEN/WILD RICE HOT DISH

Suzanne Greenslit, Merrifield, Minnesota

      1 cup uncooked wild rice
      3 cups boiling water
  2-1/2 teaspoons salt, *divided*
      1/4 cup butter or margarine
      1 pound fresh mushrooms,
        sliced
      1 medium onion, chopped
      1/4 cup minced fresh parsley
      1/4 teaspoon pepper
      3 cups diced cooked chicken
      1 jar (2 ounces) chopped
        pimiento, drained
      1 cup chicken broth
      1 cup heavy cream
      1/4 cup grated Parmesan cheese
      3/4 cup slivered almonds

Wash rice; place in a saucepan with water and 1 teaspoon salt. Cover and simmer 45-50 minutes or until tender. Drain if necessary. In a large skillet, melt butter over medium heat. Saute mushrooms, onion and parsley for 5 minutes. Stir in remaining 1-1/2 teaspoons salt, pepper, rice, chicken, pimiento, broth and cream. Place in a 13-in. x 9-in. x 2-in. baking dish. Top with cheese and almonds. Bake at 350° for 50-60 minutes. **Yield:** 8-10 servings.

BUTTER PECAN CAKE

Virginia Gentry, Sutherlin, Virginia

      3 tablespoons butter or
        margarine, melted
  1-1/3 cups chopped pecans
      2/3 cup butter or margarine,
        softened
  1-1/3 cups sugar
      2 eggs
      2 cups all-purpose flour
  1-1/2 teaspoons baking powder
      1/4 teaspoon salt
      2/3 cup milk
  1-1/2 teaspoons vanilla extract

BUTTER PECAN FROSTING:
      3 tablespoons butter or
        margarine, softened
      3 cups confectioners' sugar
      3 tablespoons milk
      3/4 teaspoon vanilla extract

Pour melted butter into a baking pan. Stir in pecans. Toast at 350° for 10 minutes. Set aside to cool. In a mixing bowl, cream butter and sugar until light and fluffy. Add eggs, one at a time, beating well after each addition. Combine flour, baking powder and salt; add to creamed mixture alternately with milk, beginning and ending with dry ingredients. Stir in vanilla and 1 cup toasted pecans. Pour batter into two greased and floured 8-in. round cake pans. Bake at 350° for 30-35 minutes or until the cakes test done. Cool in pans 5 minutes. Remove from pans and cool thoroughly on a wire rack. Meanwhile, for frosting, cream butter and sugar. Add milk and vanilla, beating until light and fluffy. Add additional milk if needed. Stir in remaining toasted pecans. Spread between the layers and over the top and sides of the cake. **Yield:** 12 servings.

AUTUMN BEANS

Mara McAuley, Hinsdale, New York

      8 slices bacon, chopped
      1/4 cup minced onion
      1 cup apple cider
      2 cans (16 ounces *each*) baked
        beans, undrained
      1/4 to 1/2 cup raisins
      1/2 teaspoon ground cinnamon

In a skillet, lightly fry bacon. Remove to paper towel to drain. Discard all but 2 tablespoons drippings. Saute onion in the drippings until tender. Add all remaining ingredients. Bring to a boil; reduce heat and simmer, uncovered, 20-25 minutes, stirring occasionally. **Yield:** 4 servings.

FROSTING FINESSE: Before frosting a cake, place strips of waxed paper on the serving plate under the bottom cake layer. After frosting, carefully remove the waxed paper—you'll have a clean plate.

• Unfrosted cake layers can be frozen on a cookie sheet until firm, wrapped separately with plastic wrap and kept in the freezer. When they're ready for use, just thaw, frost and serve.

MEALS IN MINUTES

BETWEEN RAISING a toddler of her own and caring for a neighbor's child on weekdays, Joanne Schlabach of Shreve, Ohio doesn't have many seconds to spare. So it's no wonder this busy mom and sitter is always searching for fast menus that also have "kid appeal"!

"I rely on recipes that can be prepared ahead and held until the children are settled and all set to eat," Joanne reports. "Pizza Burgers are one of their favorites. But my husband enjoys them as well!"

In fact, the Meals in Minutes menu that she shares here is truly a family affair. The zesty main dish came from her mother-in-law, the salad is from her own mother, and the dessert's from her grandmother.

From those ladies, Joanne also inherited a love of all kinds of cooking and baking. "On weekends, when I have a little more time, I prepare big meals from scratch," she says. Joanne finds time besides to garden, put up fruits and vegetables, sew and help work on the house the Schlabachs are building.

When a fast meal is in order, Joanne pulls out her skillet and stirs up some of her Pizza Burgers (an Italian-style sloppy joe). "You can make the filling ahead and reheat it when you're ready to serve," she notes.

While the filling simmers, Joanne prepares the crunchy layered salad. Then the refreshing lemon dessert is mixed in minutes and chilled while she and the children eat.

Give Joanne's finished-in-a-jiffy menu a quick try soon—it'll please everyone in your family—kids (of all ages) included!

PIZZA BURGERS

- 1 pound lean ground beef
- 1 can (15 ounces) pizza sauce
- 1 teaspoon dried oregano
- 1/2 medium onion
- 1/2 medium green pepper
- 1 ounce sliced pepperoni
- 6 hamburger buns, split
- 1/2 cup shredded Mozzarella cheese
- 1/2 cup sliced fresh mushrooms

In a skillet, brown ground beef. Drain. Stir in sauce and oregano. In a food processor, chop onion, pepper and pepperoni; add to beef mixture. Simmer 20-25 minutes. Spoon mixture onto buns. Top with cheese and mushrooms. Serve immediately. **Yield:** 6 servings.

LAYERED LETTUCE SALAD

- 1 cup mayonnaise
- 3 tablespoons grated Parmesan cheese
- 2 tablespoons sugar
- 1 medium head lettuce, torn into bite-size pieces
- 1 medium head cauliflower, broken into florets

- 1 medium red onion, thinly sliced
- 1/2 cup bacon bits

In a small bowl, stir together first three ingredients for dressing; set aside. Layer remaining ingredients in a large salad bowl. Pour on dressing; refrigerate. Toss just before serving. **Yield:** 6-8 servings.

LEMON PIE

- 1 can (14 ounces) sweetened condensed milk
- 1/2 cup lemon juice
- 1 carton (8 ounces) frozen whipped topping, thawed
- Few drops yellow food coloring, optional
- 1 prepared graham cracker crust (8 or 9 inches)

In a medium bowl, combine milk and juice. Let stand a few minutes. Stir in whipped topping. Add food coloring if desired. Spoon into crust. Chill until firm. **Yield:** 6 servings.

'My Most Memorable Meal'

When Sandra Anderson was growing up in Arnold, Nebraska in the '50's, the Fourth of July was one of the biggest holidays of the entire year.

A picnic outing with several families to a nearby river made it a big celebration. Traditions were so well-established back then that the menu for the picnic remained the same.

"Everybody who came prepared the same foods each year," Sandra recalls, "but I always thought Ma-

ma's was the best. She made potato salad the way her mother made it.

"Mama also served up the best fried chicken ever, accompanied by homemade bread-and-butter sandwiches. She topped it off with a big pan of brownies and a gallon jar of fresh lemonade."

Sandra, who now lives in New York, revives memories of those delightful picnics by preparing her mother's tasty potato salad and the other dishes shown above. For Sandra, they make up her "Most

Memorable Meal".

"When I make these recipes memories of those old-time Fourth of July celebrations come flooding back," she recounts fondly. "I re member swimming in that river enjoying that great picnic, and ending the day watching fireworks in the clear country sky."

STAR-SPANGLED SPECIALTIES
Clockwise from top right: **Homemade Bread, Fried Chicken, Chocolate Nut Brownies, Mama's Potato Salad** (a recipes on page 63).

MEMORABLE MEAL

The first four recipes listed here come from Sandra Anderson of Arnold, Nebraska (see photo and story at left).

FRIED CHICKEN

1-1/2 cups all-purpose flour
1-1/2 teaspoons salt
1/2 teaspoon pepper
1/2 teaspoon garlic powder
1 broiler/fryer chicken (2-1/2 to 3 pounds), cut up
Shortening

In a bowl, combine first four ingredients. Wash and dry chicken; coat pieces in flour mixture. In a skillet, melt shortening to 1/2-in. depth over medium-high heat. Fry chicken (in batches if necessary) in hot shortening until golden brown on all sides. Return all chicken to pan; cover and cook over low heat until chicken is done, about 30 minutes. **Yield:** about 8 servings.

HOMEMADE BREAD

✓ This tasty dish uses less sugar, salt and fat. Recipe includes *Diabetic Exchanges*.

2 packages (1/4 ounce *each*) active dry yeast
4-1/2 cups warm water (110°-115°)
6 tablespoons sugar
2 tablespoons salt
1/4 cup shortening, melted and cooled
12 to 12-1/2 cups all-purpose flour, *divided*

In a large mixing bowl, dissolve yeast in water. Add sugar, salt and shortening; stir until dissolved. Add half the flour; beat until smooth and the batter sheets with a spoon. Mix in enough remaining flour to form a soft dough that cleans the bowl. Turn onto a floured board. Knead 8-10 minutes or until smooth and elastic. Place in a greased bowl, turning once to grease top. Cover and allow to rise in a warm place until doubled, about 1-1/2 hours. Punch dough down. Cover and let rise again for 30 minutes. Divide dough into four parts and shape into loaves. Place in four greased 9-in. x 5-in. x 3-in. loaf pans. Cover and let rise in a warm place until doubled, about 30-45 minutes. Bake at 375° for 30-35 minutes or until golden brown. Remove from pans and allow to cool on wire racks. **Yield:** 4 loaves. **Diabetic Exchanges:** One serving (one slice) equals 1 starch; also, 93 calories, 70 mg sodium, 0 mg cholesterol, 18 gm carbohydrate, 3 gm protein, 1 gm fat. *If cooking for two:* Wrap and freeze whole or sliced breads.

MAMA'S POTATO SALAD

3 to 3-1/2 pounds potatoes (about 10 medium)
6 hard-cooked eggs
1 medium onion, finely chopped
1/2 cup mayonnaise
1/2 cup evaporated milk
3 tablespoons vinegar
2 tablespoons prepared mustard
1/4 cup sugar
1 teaspoon salt
1/4 teaspoon pepper
Additional hard-cooked eggs, sliced
Paprika

In a large kettle, cook potatoes in boiling salted water until tender. Drain and cool. Peel potatoes; cut into chunks. Separate egg yolks from whites. Set yolks aside. Chop whites and add to potatoes with onion. In a small bowl, mash yolks. Stir in mayonnaise, milk, vinegar, mustard, sugar, salt and pepper. Pour over potatoes; toss well. Adjust seasonings if necessary. Spoon into a serving bowl. Garnish with egg slices and paprika. Chill until serving. **Yield:** 12 servings.

CHOCOLATE NUT BROWNIES

2/3 cup shortening
2 cups sugar
4 eggs
1 teaspoon vanilla extract
3/4 cup unsweetened cocoa
1-1/2 cups all-purpose flour
1 teaspoon baking powder
1/2 teaspoon salt
1 cup chopped nuts, *divided*

In a mixing bowl, beat shortening, sugar, eggs and vanilla just until smooth. Combine dry ingredients; stir into batter. Fold in half the nuts. Spread into a greased 13-in. x 9-in. x 2-in. baking pan. Sprinkle remaining nuts on top. Bake at 350° for 20-25 minutes or until brownies pull away from the sides of the pan. Cool on wire rack. Cut into squares. **Yield:** 2 dozen.

ONION/ CUCUMBER SALAD

Dlores DeWitt, Colorado Springs, Colorado

1/4 cup vegetable oil
2 tablespoons vinegar
2 tablespoons sugar
1 tablespoon water
1/2 cup sour cream
Salt to taste
1 large cucumber, sliced
1 medium red onion, sliced

In a bowl, combine oil, vinegar, sugar, water, sour cream and salt. Add cucumber and onion; toss to coat. Refrigerate several hours or overnight. **Yield:** 4-6 servings.

SUGAR COOKIES

Helen Wallis, Vancouver, Washington

1/2 cup butter
1/2 cup shortening
1 cup sugar
1 egg
1 teaspoon vanilla extract
2-1/4 cups all-purpose flour
1/2 teaspoon baking powder
1/2 teaspoon baking soda
Additional sugar

In a mixing bowl, cream butter, shortening and sugar. Add egg and vanilla; mix well. Combine flour, baking powder and baking soda; gradually add to the creamed mixture. Shape into 1-in. balls. Roll in sugar. Place on greased cookie sheet; flatten with a glass. Bake at 350° for 10-12 minutes. **Yield:** 5 dozen.

WILTED LETTUCE

Edna Mugasis, Colorado Springs, Colorado

2 quarts fresh torn leaf lettuce
2 tablespoons sliced green onions
5 slices bacon
1/4 cup vinegar
1 teaspoon dry mustard
1-1/2 teaspoons sugar
1/4 teaspoon salt
1/4 teaspoon pepper
1/8 teaspoon garlic salt

Place lettuce and onions in a salad bowl; set aside. In a skillet, fry bacon until crisp. Remove bacon; set aside. In the drippings, combine all remaining ingredients. Bring to a boil, stirring constantly. Immediately pour over salad. Crumble bacon and add to salad; toss well. Serve immediately. **Yield:** 4 servings.

QUICK & EASY CRANBERRIES

YOU won't find yourself "bogged" down in your kitchen when you fix any of these fast cranberry recipes! Each is a proven speedy specialty of a country cook who's happy to share.

CRANBERRY APPLE RELISH

Mary Guengerich, High River, Alberta

4 cups raw cranberries
2 apples, peeled and cored
2 oranges, quartered with peel, seeded
1 lemon, quartered with peel, seeded
2-1/2 cups sugar *or* 1-1/2 cups honey

Grind cranberries, apples, oranges and lemon. Stir in sugar or honey. Refrigerate several hours or up to several days. **Yield:** about 6 cups.

CRANBERRY SWEET-AND-SOUR PORK

Gert Snyder, West Montrose, Ontario

1 can (8-3/4 ounces) pineapple tidbits, liquid drained, reserved
1 tablespoon cornstarch
1/2 cup barbecue sauce
1 cup whole-berry cranberry sauce
1 tablespoon cooking oil
1-1/2 pounds pork tenderloin, cut into 1/2-inch cubes
1/2 teaspoon salt

QUITE A STIR is quickly created by swift sweet-and-sour pork dish (recipe above).

1/4 teaspoon pepper
1 medium green pepper, cut into strips
Cooked rice or chow mein noodles

In a bowl, combine pineapple liquid and cornstarch. Stir in sauces and set aside. In a large skillet, heat oil over high heat. Add pork, salt and pepper; stir-fry for about 3 minutes or until meat is no longer pink. Add peppers and pineapple; stir-fry 2 minutes more. Stir cornstarch mixture and add to skillet. Cook, stirring constantly, over medium-high heat, until thickened. Serve over rice or noodles. **Yield:** 6 servings.

BAKED CRANBERRY SAUCE

Marian Ridgeway, Muskegon, Michigan

2 cups fresh *or* frozen cranberries
1 cup packed brown sugar
1/4 teaspoon ground cloves

Place cranberries in a 1-qt. baking dish. Sprinkle with brown sugar and cloves. Bake, covered, at 350° for 30-35 minutes. Stir after 15 minutes. **Yield:** 1-1/2 cups.

CRANBERRY BAKED BEANS

Creacle Baxter, Yuma, Arizona

1 can (16 ounces) jellied cranberry sauce
1 can (8 ounces) tomato sauce
2 cans (31 ounces *each*) pork and beans, undrained
1 tablespoon prepared mustard
1/2 cup chopped onion
6 strips bacon, halved
3 tablespoons brown sugar

In a large bowl, combine the cranberry sauce, tomato sauce, beans, mustard and onion. Place in a greased 13-in. x 9-in. x 2-in. baking dish. Lay bacon on top. Sprinkle with brown sugar. Bake at 350° for 1 hour. **Yield:** 12-16 servings.

APPLES, BERRIES AND YAMS

Dixy Moore, Avalon, California

2 tablespoons butter *or* margarine
3 apples, peeled and cut into

chunks
1 can (23 ounces) yams, drained
1/2 teaspoon ground nutmeg
1 can (16 ounces) whole-berry cranberry sauce
1/2 cup orange marmalade

In a skillet, melt butter over medium heat. Saute apples until crisp-tender. Place apples and yams in a greased 3-qt. casserole. Sprinkle with the nutmeg. Combine cranberry sauce and marmalade. Spoon over yams. Bake at 350° for 30 minutes. **Yield:** 8-10 servings.

HOT AND SPICY CRANBERRY DIP

Dorothy Pritchett, Wills Point, Texas

1 can (16 ounces) jellied cranberry sauce
2 to 3 tablespoons prepared horseradish
2 tablespoons honey
1 tablespoon Worcestershire sauce
1 tablespoon lemon juice
1 garlic clove, minced
1/4 to 1/2 teaspoon ground cayenne pepper
Pineapple chunks
Orange sections
Mini precooked sausages, warmed

In a medium saucepan, combine first seven ingredients. Bring to a boil. Reduce heat and simmer, covered, 5 minutes. Serve warm with pineapple, oranges and sausages. **Yield:** 2 cups.

CRANBERRY SLOPPY JOES

Alice Davis, Wilmington, Delaware

1 pound ground beef
1 cup chopped celery
1 cup chopped onion
1 can (10-3/4 ounces) condensed tomato soup, undiluted
1 can (8 ounces) jellied cranberry sauce
1/2 teaspoon salt
1/4 teaspoon chili powder
Dash hot pepper sauce
Hamburger buns, split and toasted

In a skillet, cook beef, celery and onion until meat is brown and vegetables are tender. Drain. Stir in soup, cranberry sauce, salt, chili powder and hot pepper sauce. Simmer, uncovered, about 30 minutes, stirring occasionally. Spoon onto buns. **Yield:** 8 servings.

With their lively tart taste and crimson color, there's little wonder about why cranberries long have had a place reserved on countless families' Thanksgiving and Christmas tables.

So it isn't surprising these days to see this cheerfully bright fruit becoming a standby of country cooks no matter what the season! The cranberry can be enjoyed in so many forms—as is proved here and on the pages that follow.

Cranberries are delicious in desserts, of course… but there's also a fresh new main dish to add to your recipe file plus a truly different side dish. And that's just the start. Red-y? Dig in!

VINE'S FINEST. Clockwise from top: Rich Cranberry Coffee Cake, Cranberry/Orange Chicken, Cranberry Nut Swirls, Cranberry Stuffing Balls (all recipes on page 69).

Pucker up for the pleasing, tart taste of cranberry in a variety of year-round recipes. Enjoy summer's cool Cranberry Sherbet or winter's Spicy Cranberry Warmer …try the Holiday Cranberry Jam with muffins or biscuits…or feast on a country favorite—Cranberry Meatballs. All of these cranberry dishes are bound to become popular among your family and friends. Whip up a cranberry creation today!

DANDY CRANBERRY! Clockwise from lower left: **Cranberry Chutney** (p. 69), **Cranberry Meatballs** (p. 69), **Cranberry Upside-Down Cake** (p. 70), **Cranberry Sherbet** (p. 70), **Cran-Apple Sauce** (p. 70), **Spicy Cranberry Warmer** (p. 70), **Cranberry Walnut Tart** (p. 70), **Holiday Cranberry Jam** (p. 71).

T reat family or drop-in guests to some good country cooking that's guaranteed to hit the spot. Emily's Bean Soup freezes well and makes a quick, convenient meal with thick slices of crusty fresh bread. Or pass around a plate of hot Italian Beef Sandwiches and serve up healthy portions of California Pasta Salad. Enjoy!

COUNTRY CLASSICS. Top to bottom: **Emily's Bean Soup, Italian Beef Sandwiches, California Pasta Salad** (all recipes on page 71).

RICH CRANBERRY COFFEE CAKE

Mildred Schwartzentruber, Tavistock, Ontario

(PICTURED ON PAGE 65)

1 package (8 ounces) cream
  cheese, softened
1 cup butter *or* margarine
1-1/2 cups sugar
1-1/2 teaspoons vanilla extract
4 eggs
2-1/4 cups all-purpose flour,
  divided
1-1/2 teaspoons baking powder
1/2 teaspoon salt
2 cups fresh *or* frozen
  cranberries, patted dry
1/2 cup chopped pecans *or*
  walnuts
Confectioners' sugar

In a mixing bowl, beat cream cheese, butter, sugar and vanilla until smooth. Add eggs, one at a time, mixing well after each addition. Combine 2 cups flour, baking powder and salt; gradually add to butter mixture. Mix remaining flour with cranberries and nuts; fold into batter. Batter will be very thick. Spoon into a greased 10-in. fluted tube pan. Bake at 350° for 65-70 minutes or until cake tests done. Let stand 5 minutes before removing from the pan. Cool on a wire rack. Before serving, dust with confectioners' sugar. **Yield:** about 16 servings.

CRANBERRY/ORANGE CHICKEN

Sharon Parsons, Killingworth, Connecticut

(PICTURED ON PAGE 65)

1/2 cup all-purpose flour
1/8 teaspoon salt
1 broiler/fryer chicken
  (about 3 pounds), cut up
4 tablespoons butter *or*
  margarine
2 cups whole fresh *or* frozen
  cranberries
1/2 cup chopped onion
2 tablespoons grated orange
  peel
1-3/4 cups sugar
1-1/4 cups orange juice
1/4 teaspoon ground ginger
1/4 teaspoon ground cinnamon
Red food coloring, optional

Combine the flour and salt and place in a plastic bag. Shake chicken, a few pieces at a time, in flour mixture. Melt butter in a large skillet; brown chicken on all sides. In a saucepan, combine remaining ingredients except food coloring; bring to a boil and pour over chick-

en. Cover and simmer 1 hour. Remove chicken to a warm platter. Bring sauce to a boil and cook, stirring constantly, until thickened. Add a few drops red food coloring if desired. Serve sauce over chicken. **Yield:** 4-6 servings.

CRANBERRY NUT SWIRLS

Carla Hodenfield, Mandan, North Dakota

(PICTURED ON PAGE 65)

1/2 cup butter *or* margarine,
  softened
3/4 cup sugar
1 egg
1 teaspoon vanilla extract
1-1/2 cups all-purpose flour
1/4 teaspoon baking powder
1/4 teaspoon salt
1/2 cup finely ground cranberries
1/2 cup finely chopped walnuts
1 tablespoon grated orange peel
3 tablespoons brown sugar
2 teaspoons milk

In a large mixing bowl, combine first four ingredients. Beat until light and fluffy, scraping the bowl occasionally. Combine dry ingredients; add to the creamed mixture. Refrigerate at least 1 hour. In a small bowl, combine cranberries, walnuts and orange peel; set aside. On a lightly floured surface, roll dough into a 10-in. square. Combine brown sugar and milk; spread over the dough. Sprinkle with the cranberry mixture, leaving about a 1/2-in. edge at both ends of dough; roll up tightly, jelly-roll style. Wrap with waxed paper; chill several hours or overnight. Cut roll into 1/4-in. slices and place on well-greased cookie sheets. Bake at 375° for 14-15 minutes or until edges are light brown. **Yield:** about 3-1/2 dozen.

CRANBERRY STUFFING BALLS

Bernadine Dirmeyer, Harpster, Ohio

(PICTURED ON PAGE 65)

1 pound bulk pork sausage
1/2 cup chopped celery
1/4 cup chopped onion
2 tablespoons minced fresh
  parsley
1 package (7 ounces) herb-
  seasoned stuffing croutons
3/4 cup fresh cranberries, halved
2 eggs, well beaten
1 to 1-1/2 cups chicken broth

In a skillet, cook sausage, celery and onion until sausage is done and vegetables are tender. Drain excess fat. In

a large mixing bowl, combine the meat mixture with remaining ingredients and enough broth to hold mixture together. Shape into 8-10 balls. Place in a greased shallow baking dish. Bake at 325° for 30 minutes. **Yield:** 8-10 servings.

CRANBERRY CHUTNEY

Joyce Vivian, Mitchell, Ontario

(PICTURED ON PAGE 66)

3 cups fresh *or* frozen
  cranberries
1 cup chopped dried apricots
1/2 cup chopped dates
1/2 cup chopped onion
1/2 cup cider vinegar
1/2 cup light corn syrup
3/4 cup packed brown sugar
1 tablespoon grated orange peel
3/4 cup orange juice
1/2 teaspoon dry mustard
1/2 teaspoon salt
1/4 teaspoon ground ginger

In a large heavy saucepan, combine all ingredients. Bring to a boil. Reduce heat and simmer, uncovered, for 15-20 minutes or until thickened and cranberries have popped. Chill. Serve as an accompaniment to turkey or pork. **Yield:** about 3-1/2 cups.

CRANBERRY MEATBALLS

Tammy Neubauer, Ida Grove, Iowa

(PICTURED ON PAGE 66)

MEATBALLS:
2 eggs, beaten
1 cup cornflake crumbs
1/3 cup ketchup
2 tablespoons soy sauce
1 tablespoon dried parsley flakes
2 tablespoons dehydrated onion
1/2 teaspoon salt
1/4 teaspoon pepper
2 pounds ground pork
SAUCE:
1 can (16 ounces) jellied
  cranberry sauce
1 cup ketchup
3 tablespoons brown sugar
1 tablespoon lemon juice

In a mixing bowl, combine meatball ingredients. Shape into 72 meatballs (1 in. each). Place in a 15-in. x 10-in. x 1-in. baking pan. Bake at 350° for 20-25 minutes or until done. Remove from the oven; drain on paper towels. In a large saucepan, combine sauce ingredients. Cook, stirring frequently, until the cranberry sauce is melted. Add the meatballs and heat through. **Yield:** 12 main-dish or 24 appetizer servings.

SPICY CRANBERRY WARMER

Marlene Cartwright, Sierra City, California

(PICTURED ON PAGE 67)

3 whole cloves
2 cinnamon sticks
2 whole allspice
4 cups apple cider
1/3 cup packed brown sugar
4 cups cranberry juice
Additional cinnamon sticks, optional

Place first three ingredients in a double thickness of cheesecloth. Bring up corners of cloth and tie with a string. Place with cider in a large saucepan. (Or, if desired, place loose spices in saucepan and strain before serving.) Simmer, covered, for 5 minutes. Stir in sugar and simmer for 5 minutes. Add cranberry juice and heat to simmering temperature. Serve hot in mugs. Garnish with cinnamon sticks if desired. **Yield:** 8-10 servings.

CRAN-APPLE SAUCE

Stella Kalynchuk, Whitehorse, Yukon Territory

(PICTURED ON PAGE 67)

1 cup fresh *or* frozen cranberries
6 large apples, peeled, cored and coarsely chopped
1/2 cup sugar
1/3 cup apple juice
1/4 teaspoon ground mace
1/8 teaspoon ground coriander

In a large saucepan, combine all ingredients. Bring to a boil. Reduce heat; cover and simmer for 10-15 minutes or until apples are tender. Remove from heat and cool slightly. Puree mixture in food processor. Cover and refrigerate. **Yield:** about 4 cups.

CRANBERRY SHERBET

Heather Clement, Indian River, Ontario

(PICTURED ON PAGE 67)

1 bag (12 ounces) fresh *or* frozen cranberries
2-3/4 cups water, *divided*
2 cups sugar
1 envelope unflavored gelatin
1/2 cup orange juice

In a saucepan, combine cranberries and 2-1/2 cups of water. Bring to a boil; cook gently until all the cranberries have popped, about 10 minutes. Remove from heat; cool slightly. Press mixture through a sieve or food mill, reserving juice and discarding skins and seeds. In another saucepan, combine cranberry juice and sugar; cook over medium heat until the sugar dissolves. Remove from the heat and set aside. Combine gelatin and remaining 1/4 cup water; stir until softened. Combine cranberry mixture, orange juice and gelatin; mix well. Pour into a 2-qt. container; freeze 4-5 hours or until mixture is slushy. Remove from freezer; beat with electric mixer until sherbet is a bright pink color. Freeze until firm. **Yield:** about 6 cups.

CRANBERRY WALNUT TART

Beverly Mix, Missoula, Montana

(PICTURED ON PAGE 67)

TART SHELL:
1 cup all-purpose flour
1/3 cup sugar
Dash salt
5 tablespoons butter *or* margarine
1 egg, lightly beaten
1/2 tablespoon water, optional
FILLING:
1/2 cup sugar
1/2 cup light corn syrup
2 eggs, lightly beaten
2 tablespoons butter *or* margarine, melted
1 teaspoon grated orange peel
1 cup walnut halves
1 cup fresh *or* frozen cranberries

In a large bowl, combine flour, sugar and salt. With a pastry blender, cut in butter until mixture resembles very coarse crumbs. Add egg and stir lightly with fork just until mixture forms a ball, adding the water if necessary. Wrap in waxed paper and refrigerate at least 1 hour. Grease a 9-in. fluted tart pan with removable bottom. Press chilled pastry into the bottom and up the sides of pan. Line pastry shell with foil; fill with pie weights, raw rice or beans to prevent shrinkage. Bake at 375° for 10 minutes. Remove weights and bake another 5 minutes. Cool. Meanwhile, for filling, combine sugar, syrup, eggs, butter and peel in a large bowl; set aside. Place walnuts and cranberries in bottom of tart; pour sugar mixture into pan. Bake for 30-35 minutes or until crust is golden, edge of filling is firm and center is almost set. Cool on wire rack. Chill until serving. Store leftovers in the refrigerator. **Yield:** 12 servings.

CRANBERRY UPSIDE-DOWN CAKE

Doris Heath, Bryson City, North Carolina

(PICTURED ON PAGE 66)

1/2 cup butter *or* margarine
2 cups sugar, *divided*
1 can (16 ounces) whole-berry cranberry sauce
1/2 cup coarsely chopped pecans
3 eggs, *separated*
1/3 cup orange juice
1 cup all-purpose flour
1 teaspoon baking powder
1/4 teaspoon salt

Melt butter in a 10-in. iron skillet. Add 1 cup sugar; cook and stir 3 minutes over medium heat. Remove from heat. Spoon cranberry sauce over butter mixture; sprinkle pecans over all. Set aside. In a mixing bowl, beat egg yolks until foamy. Gradually add remaining sugar; beat well. Blend in orange juice. Combine flour, baking powder and salt; add to egg mixture. Beat egg whites until stiff; fold into batter. Carefully spoon over topping in skillet. Bake at 375° about 30 minutes or until cake tests done. Cool 5 minutes in skillet; invert onto large serving plate. Serve warm. **Yield:** 10 servings.

SOUTHWESTERN SWISS STEAK

Myra Innes, Auburn, Kansas

1 pound round steak, cut into serving-size pieces
1/4 teaspoon salt
1/8 teaspoon pepper
2 tablespoons all-purpose flour
1 tablespoon cooking oil
10 onion slices
1 garlic clove, minced
1 can (16 ounces) tomatoes with liquid, chopped
1/4 cup mild, medium *or* hot picante sauce
1/4 cup beef broth

Sprinkle meat with salt and pepper. Using a mallet, pound all of the flour into the meat. In a skillet, heat oil over medium-high. Brown the meat on both sides. Arrange onion slices over the meat. Combine remaining ingredients and pour over onions. Cover and simmer until the meat is tender, about 45 minutes. Remove meat and keep warm. Cook the sauce until it is reduced and thickened, about 5 minutes. Season to taste with additional salt and pepper if desired. Pour sauce over meat and serve immediately. **Yield:** 4 servings.

HOLIDAY CRANBERRY JAM

Sandee Berg, Fort Saskatchewan, Alberta

(PICTURED ON PAGE 66)

2 cups fresh *or* frozen
  cranberries
1 medium orange, peeled and
  broken into sections
1 carton (16 ounces) frozen
  sliced strawberries, thawed
3 cups sugar
1/2 of a 6-ounce package liquid
  fruit pectin

In a food grinder or food processor, coarsely grind cranberries and orange sections. Place in a Dutch oven or large kettle with strawberries and sugar. Bring to a full rolling boil over high heat, stirring constantly. Boil for 1 minute. Remove from the heat and stir in the pectin. Quickly skim off the foam with a large metal spoon. Immediately pour into hot sterilized jars. Adjust caps. Process 10 minutes in a boiling-water bath. **Yield:** 5 half-pints.

EMILY'S BEAN SOUP

Emily Chaney, Penobscot, Maine

(PICTURED ON PAGE 68)

1/2 cup *each* great northern
  beans, kidney beans, navy
  beans, lima beans, butter
  beans, split green *or* yellow
  peas, pinto beans and lentils
Water
1 ham bone
2 chicken bouillon cubes
1 can (28 ounces) tomatoes
  with liquid, quartered
1 can (6 ounces) tomato paste
1 large onion, chopped
3 celery stalks, chopped
4 carrots, sliced
2 garlic cloves, minced
1/4 cup dried chives
3 bay leaves
2 tablespoons dried parsley
1 teaspoon dried thyme
1 teaspoon dry mustard
1/2 teaspoon ground red *or*
  cayenne pepper

Wash all beans thoroughly; drain and place in a 4-qt. kettle with 5 cups of water. Bring to a rapid boil; boil 2 minutes. Remove from heat and let stand, covered, for 1 hour. Meanwhile, place ham bone and 3 qts. of water in an 8-qt. soup kettle. Simmer until beans have stood for 1 hour. Drain beans and add to the ham stock; add remaining ingredients. Simmer 2-3 hours or until beans are tender. Discard bone; add

additional water if desired. **Yield:** about 5-1/2 quarts.

ITALIAN BEEF SANDWICHES

Marjorie Libby, Madison, Wisconsin

(PICTURED ON PAGE 68)

1 beef sirloin tip roast (4 to 5
  pounds)
Water
1/2 teaspoon salt
2 to 3 onions, thinly sliced
1 teaspoon onion salt
1 teaspoon garlic salt
1 teaspoon dried oregano
2 teaspoons Italian seasoning
1 teaspoon seasoned salt
1 teaspoon dried basil
3 beef bouillon cubes
7 to 8 hot banana peppers,
  seeded and sliced
Hard rolls

In a deep baking pan, place roast and 1 in. of water. Sprinkle with salt and cover with onions. Bake, covered, at 350° for 1-1/2 hours or until meat is tender. Remove meat from baking pan; reserve and chill broth. Refrigerate meat until firm. Cut into thin slices. Place in a 13-in. x 9-in. x 2-in. baking pan; set aside. Meanwhile, in a saucepan, combine broth with remaining ingredients except rolls. Bring to a boil; reduce heat and simmer 10 minutes. Pour over meat. Cover and refrigerate for 24 hours. Reheat, covered, at 325° for 1 hour. Serve on hard rolls. **Yield:** 20-24 sandwiches.

CALIFORNIA PASTA SALAD

Jeanette Krembas, Laguna Niguel, California

(PICTURED ON PAGE 68)

1 pound thin spaghetti *or*
  vermicelli, broken into 1-inch
  pieces, cooked
3 large tomatoes, diced
2 medium zucchini, diced
1 large cucumber, diced
1 medium green pepper, diced
1 sweet red pepper, diced
1 large red onion, diced
2 cans (2-1/4 ounces *each)* sliced
  ripe olives, drained
1 bottle (16 ounces) Italian
  salad dressing
1/4 cup grated Parmesan *or*
  Romano cheese
1 tablespoon sesame seeds
2 teaspoons poppy seeds
1 teaspoon paprika
1/2 teaspoon celery seed

1/4 teaspoon garlic powder

Combine all ingredients in a large bowl; cover with plastic wrap and refrigerate overnight to blend flavors. **Yield:** 10-15 servings.

ZUCCHINI CHUTNEY

Marilou Robinson, Portland, Oregon

2 pounds small zucchini
1 tart apple, peeled and cored
1 medium onion
1 green pepper
1 garlic clove, minced
1-1/2 cups packed brown sugar
1 cup vinegar
1 jar (2 ounces) chopped
  pimiento, drained
1 tablespoon finely minced
  fresh gingerroot
1 tablespoon Dijon mustard
1/4 to 1/2 teaspoon crushed red
  pepper flakes
1/2 teaspoon salt

Peel zucchini and discard any large seeds; chop into small pieces (about 5 cups). Finely chop apple, onion and green pepper; place in a Dutch oven along with zucchini and remaining ingredients. Bring to a boil. Reduce heat and simmer, uncovered, over medium heat until thick, about 45-55 minutes, stirring often. Cool. Ladle into jars; cover and refrigerate. **Yield:** about 3-1/2 cups.

TUNA ZUCCHINI CAKES

Billie Blanton, Kingsport, Tennessee

1 tablespoon butter *or*
  margarine
1/2 cup finely diced onion
1 can (6-1/8 ounces) tuna,
  drained and flaked
1 cup shredded zucchini
2 eggs, lightly beaten
1/3 cup snipped fresh parsley
1 teaspoon lemon juice
1/2 teaspoon salt
1/8 teaspoon pepper
1 cup seasoned bread crumbs,
  divided
2 tablespoons cooking oil

In a small saucepan, melt butter. Cook the onion until tender, but not brown. Remove from the heat. Add tuna, zucchini, eggs, parsley, lemon juice, seasonings and 1/2 cup bread crumbs. Stir until well combined. Shape into six 1/2-in.-thick patties; coat with remaining bread crumbs. In a medium skillet, heat oil and cook the patties 3 minutes on each side or until golden brown. **Yield:** 3 servings.

71

NUTMEG SAUCED APPLES

Helen Bridges, Washington, Virginia

6 medium tart baking apples, peeled, cored and halved
1/3 cup water
4 teaspoons sugar
4 teaspoons all-purpose flour
1/2 teaspoon ground nutmeg
1-1/2 cups light cream

Place apples in a 13-in. x 9-in. x 2-in. baking dish; add water. Bake, covered, at 350° for 30-40 minutes or until tender. Remove from the oven and keep warm. In a small saucepan, combine sugar, flour and nutmeg. Stir in cream. Cook and stir over medium heat until thickened and bubbly. Cook 2 minutes longer. Remove from the heat. Serve warm over apples. **Yield:** 6 servings.

AUTUMN FRUIT SALAD

Kathryn Booher, Laguna Hills, California

1-1/2 cups sugar
1/2 cup all-purpose flour
1-1/2 cups water
1 teaspoon butter *or* margarine
1 teaspoon vanilla extract
6 cups cubed unpeeled apples
2 cups halved red seedless grapes
1 cup diced celery
1 cup walnut halves

In a saucepan, combine sugar and flour. Stir in water; bring to a boil. Cook and stir until mixture thickens. Remove from the heat; stir in butter and vanilla. Cool to room temperature. In a large bowl, combine apples, grapes, celery and walnuts. Add dressing; toss gently. Refrigerate until serving. **Yield:** 8-10 servings.

BEEF AND SAUSAGE SOUP

Darlene Dickinson, Lebec, California

1 tablespoon cooking oil
1 pound beef stew meat, cut into 1/2-inch cubes
1 pound bulk Italian sausage, shaped into balls
1 can (28 ounces) tomatoes with liquid, chopped
3-1/2 cups water
1 cup chopped onion
1 teaspoon salt
1/2 teaspoon Italian seasoning

1 tablespoon Worcestershire sauce
2 cups cubed peeled potatoes
1 cup sliced celery

In a Dutch oven, heat oil over medium-high. Brown beef on all sides. Remove with a slotted spoon and set aside. Brown sausage on all sides. Drain fat. Return beef to Dutch oven and add remaining ingredients except potatoes and celery. Bring to a boil; reduce heat and simmer, covered, until beef is tender, about 1-1/2 hours. Add the potatoes and celery. Simmer, covered, until vegetables are tender, about 30 minutes. **Yield:** 6-8 servings.

FRENCH DRESSING WITH TOMATOES

Dana Barnes, Beaufort, South Carolina

1 can (10-3/4 ounces) tomato soup, undiluted
1 cup vegetable oil
1/2 cup vinegar
1/2 cup sugar
1 tablespoon Worcestershire sauce
1 tablespoon prepared mustard
2 to 3 teaspoons pepper
1 teaspoon salt
1/4 teaspoon garlic powder
Tomatoes, cut into wedges
Lettuce leaves

In a jar or airtight container, place all ingredients except last two. Shake well. In a bowl, place tomatoes and enough dressing to cover. Let stand several hours at room temperature. To serve, remove tomatoes from dressing with a slotted spoon; place on lettuce leaves. Drizzle with dressing. **Yield:** 3 cups dressing. *If cooking for two:* Prepare dressing and store in the refrigerator to use in small portions for several weeks.

CORN PUDDING

Peggy Burdick, Burlington, Michigan

4 tablespoons butter *or* margarine, *divided*
1 green pepper, chopped
1 medium onion, chopped
3 tablespoons all-purpose flour
1 teaspoon salt
Dash pepper
1-1/2 cups milk
3 egg yolks, lightly beaten
2 cups fresh *or* frozen corn kernels
2 jars (2 ounces *each*) chopped pimientos, drained
1-2/3 cups cracker crumbs, *divided*

In a skillet, melt 3 tablespoons butter over medium heat. Saute pepper and onion until tender. Add flour, salt and pepper; stir until well blended. Gradually add milk; cook and stir until thickened. Slowly blend in egg yolks. Remove from the heat; fold in corn, pimientos and 1 cup crumbs. Pour into a greased 1-1/2-qt. casserole. Melt remaining butter and toss with remaining crumbs; sprinkle over casserole. Bake, uncovered, at 350° for 30-40 minutes. **Yield:** 6 servings.

ANGEL FOOD CAKE

Lucille Proctor, Panguitch, Utah

1-1/2 cups egg whites (about 1 dozen), room temperature
1-1/2 teaspoons cream of tartar
1-1/2 teaspoons vanilla extract
1/2 teaspoon almond extract
1/4 teaspoon salt
1 cup sugar
1 cup confectioners' sugar
1 cup all-purpose flour

In a mixing bowl, beat egg whites, cream of tartar, extracts and salt at high speed. While beating, gradually add sugar; beat until sugar is dissolved and mixture forms stiff peaks. Combine confectioners' sugar and flour; gradually fold into the batter, 1/4 cup at a time. Gently spoon mixture into an *ungreased* 10-in. tube pan. With a metal spatula or knife, cut through the batter to break large air pockets. Bake at 350° for about 35 minutes or until cake springs back when lightly touched. Immediately invert cake in pan to cool completely. When cool, remove from pan. **Yield:** 16 servings. *If cooking for two:* Freeze individual slices for quick desserts.

SAVORY MEATBALLS

Delores Jordan, Oregon, Illinois

2 eggs, lightly beaten
1 medium onion, chopped
2 teaspoons dry mustard
1 teaspoon salt
1/2 teaspoon pepper
1/2 teaspoon poultry seasoning
1/3 cup cornmeal
3/4 cup milk
2 pounds ground beef
3 tablespoons shortening
2 cans (10-3/4 ounces *each*) cream of mushroom soup, undiluted
1-1/2 cups water

In a mixing bowl, combine the first eight ingredients. Add beef and mix well. Shape into 2-in. balls. In a skillet, melt the shortening over medium-high heat.

Brown meatballs. Place in a casserole dish. Combine soup and water; pour over meatballs. Bake, uncovered, at 350° for 45-50 minutes. **Yield:** about 8 servings.

BEEF AND NOODLE CASSEROLE

Mary Hinman, Escondido, California

1-1/2 pounds ground beef
1 tablespoon butter *or* margarine
1 large onion, chopped
1 cup chopped green pepper
1 tablespoon Worcestershire sauce
1 package (10 ounces) wide noodles, cooked and drained
2 cans (10-3/4 ounces *each*) cream of tomato soup, undiluted
1 can (10-3/4 ounces) cream of mushroom soup, undiluted
1 cup (4 ounces) shredded cheddar cheese

In a large skillet, brown beef. Remove beef and drain fat. In the same skillet, melt butter over medium-high heat. Saute onion and pepper until tender. Add beef, Worcestershire sauce, noodles and soups; mix well. Spoon into a greased 3-qt. casserole; top with cheese. Bake at 350° for 45 minutes. **Yield:** 8 servings.

POTATO/CUCUMBER SOUP

Janet Flower, Portland, Oregon

3 cups cold water
6 medium potatoes (about 2 pounds), peeled and cubed
1-1/2 teaspoons salt
1/4 teaspoon pepper
1 cup heavy cream
1 cup milk
1 teaspoon grated onion
1 large *or* 2 medium cucumbers, peeled, seeded and diced
1 tablespoon finely chopped fresh dill *or* 1 teaspoon dried dill weed

In a large saucepan, bring water, potatoes, salt and pepper to a boil. Reduce heat to simmer. Cook, uncovered, until potatoes are tender. Cool. Puree in a food processor or blender until smooth. Return to the saucepan. Stir in cream, milk, onion and cucumber. Add additional milk if soup is too thick. Simmer over low heat, stirring occasionally, for 5 minutes. Season with dill. **Yield:** 2 quarts.

RAISIN SPICE CAKE

Nancy Johnson, Milton, Pennsylvania

2 cups raisins
1-1/2 cups water
1/2 cup shortening
2 cups packed brown sugar
3 cups all-purpose flour
1 teaspoon ground cinnamon
1 teaspoon ground cloves
1/4 teaspoon ground nutmeg
1/2 teaspoon salt
1 cup buttermilk *or* sour milk
1 teaspoon baking soda
3 eggs, beaten
Confectioners' sugar

In a saucepan, combine raisins and water. Cook until plump. Drain and set aside raisins, reserving 10 tablespoons cooking liquid. In a mixing bowl, cream shortening and sugar. Combine flour, cinnamon, cloves, nutmeg and salt; set aside. Combine milk, soda, eggs and reserved cooking liquid. Add dry ingredients alternately with milk mixture to creamed mixture. Stir in cooked raisins. Pour into a greased 13-in. x 9-in. x 2-in. baking pan. Bake at 350° for 35-40 minutes or until cake tests done. Cool on a wire rack. Just before serving, sprinkle with confectioners' sugar. **Yield:** 12-15 servings.

CRANBERRY NUT BREAD

Virginia Jung, Janesville, Wisconsin

2 cups all-purpose flour
1/4 teaspoon salt
1-1/2 teaspoons baking powder
1/2 teaspoon soda
1 cup sugar
1 egg, beaten
2 tablespoons melted butter *or* margarine
1/2 cup orange juice
2 tablespoons hot water
1/2 pound cranberries, cut in half
1/2 cup whole pecans
Peel of an orange, grated

In a mixing bowl, combine all dry ingredients. Make a well and add the egg, butter, juice and water. Stir until dry ingredients are moistened. Fold in cranberries, nuts and orange peel. Bake in a greased 9-in. x 5-in. loaf pan

> **BERRY SMART:** Fresh cranberries are much easier to grind in a food processor or a food grinder if you freeze them first. Allow ground berries to drain well before using.

at 325° for about 1 hour or until the bread tests done. Cool 10 minutes before removing from the pan to a wire rack. **Yield:** 1 loaf. (Note: Recipe doubles well.)

HARVEST HAMBURGER CASSEROLE

Grace Hagen, Raggen, Colorado

1 pound lean ground beef, browned and drained
1 cup minced onion
1 can (28 ounces) tomatoes with liquid, cut up
1 tablespoon Worcestershire sauce
1 teaspoon salt
2 cups sliced potatoes
1/3 cup all-purpose flour
1 package (10 ounces) frozen corn, thawed
1 package (10 ounces) frozen lima beans, thawed
1 green pepper, cut into strips
1-1/2 cups (6 ounces) shredded cheddar cheese

In a mixing bowl, combine beef, onion, tomatoes with liquid, Worcestershire sauce and salt. Spoon into a greased 3-qt. casserole. Layer the potatoes, flour, corn, lima beans and green pepper on top. Bake, covered, at 375° for 45 minutes. Sprinkle with cheese and continue baking, uncovered, for 30 minutes. **Yield:** 8 servings.

BREAD-AND-BUTTER PICKLES

Olivia Miller, Memphis, Tennessee

16 cups sliced cucumbers (about 4 pounds)
6 cups thinly sliced onions
1/2 cup salt
Ice cubes
5 cups sugar
5 cups cider vinegar
1-1/2 teaspoons turmeric
1-1/2 teaspoons celery seed
1-1/2 teaspoons mustard seed

Combine cucumber and onion slices in a large bowl. Layer with salt; cover with ice cubes. Let stand 1-1/2 hours. Drain and rinse. Place remaining ingredients in a kettle and bring to a boil. Add cucumbers and onions. Return to a boil. Pack hot into hot jars to within 1/4 in. of top. Remove any air bubbles. Adjust caps. Process 15 minutes in boiling-water bath. **Yield:** about 6 pints.

'My Most Memorable Meal'

This meal stands out the most among my childhood memories because it seems to speak of my area of the country," says Helen Bridges of Washington, Virginia.

"My fondest memories are entwined with the big country kitchen in our old farmhouse. My mom cooked some absolutely delicious meals in that kitchen on her cast-iron wood stove. The meal I present here is one she cooked quite often, and when I prepare it, it takes me back to that farm and those happy days."

SENTIMENTAL MEAL. Clockwise from right: **Country Ham and Potatoes, Fried Green Tomatoes, Lettuce with Cream Dressing** (all recipes on page 75).

COUNTRY HAM AND POTATOES

2 to 3 tablespoons butter *or* margarine
2 pounds fully cooked sliced ham (about 1/2 inch thick)
1-1/2 pounds potatoes, peeled, quartered and cooked
Snipped fresh parsley

In a large heavy skillet, melt butter over medium-high heat. Brown ham on both sides. Move ham to one side of the skillet; brown potatoes in the drippings. Sprinkle potatoes with parsley. **Yield:** 6 servings.

LETTUCE WITH CREAM DRESSING

8 cups torn leaf *or* iceberg lettuce
1/2 cup sugar
1/4 cup vinegar
1/3 to 1/2 cup light cream *or* sour cream
2 to 3 tablespoons sliced green onions

Place lettuce in a large bowl. In a small bowl, stir together sugar, vinegar and light cream or sour cream until sugar dissolves and dressing is smooth. Stir in green onion. Just before serving, pour over lettuce; toss lightly. **Yield:** 6 servings.

FRIED GREEN TOMATOES

1 tablespoon brown sugar
1 cup all-purpose flour
4 to 6 medium green tomatoes, sliced 1/2 inch thick
1 egg, beaten
1/4 cup milk
1 cup seasoned dry bread crumbs
3 tablespoons butter *or* margarine
1 tablespoon cooking oil

Combine sugar and flour; place on a shallow plate. Dip both sides of each tomato slice into the mixture. Combine the egg and milk. Dip each tomato slice; then dip into the bread crumbs. In a skillet, heat butter and oil over medium-high. Fry tomatoes until brown on both sides, but firm enough to hold their shape. **Yield:** about 6 servings.

GRANDMA'S POULTRY DRESSING

Norma Howland, Joliet, Illinois

1 pound bulk pork sausage
2 eggs, lightly beaten
1 cup milk, scalded
7 cups coarse dry bread crumbs
2 tablespoons diced onion
1 cup diced celery
2 to 3 tablespoons minced fresh parsley
1/2 teaspoon salt *or* salt to taste

In a skillet, brown sausage. Drain and discard the drippings. In a large mixing bowl, combine sausage and remaining ingredients; mix well. Place in a greased 2-qt. casserole. Bake, covered, at 350° for 40 minutes or until lightly browned. **Yield:** 6 cups (makes enough to stuff a medium-size turkey).

APPLE BUTTER COOKIES

Dorothy Hawkins, Springhill, Florida

1/4 cup butter *or* margarine, softened
1 cup packed brown sugar
1 egg
1/2 cup quick-cooking oats
1/2 cup apple butter
1 cup all-purpose flour
1/2 teaspoon baking soda
1/2 teaspoon baking powder
1/2 teaspoon salt
2 tablespoons milk
1/2 cup chopped nuts
1/2 cup raisins

In a mixing bowl, cream butter and sugar. Beat in egg, oats and apple butter. Combine dry ingredients; gradually add to creamed mixture along with the milk; beat until blended. Stir in nuts and raisins. Chill well. Drop by teaspoonfuls onto lightly greased cookie sheets. Bake at 350° for 15 minutes. **Yield:** about 2-1/2 dozen. *If cooking for two:* Freeze baked cookies in tins or freezer bags for the months ahead.

POPPY SEED CHICKEN

Ernestin Plasek, Houston, Texas

1 tablespoon butter *or* margarine
8 ounces sliced fresh mushrooms
5 cups cubed cooked chicken
1 can (10-3/4 ounces) cream of chicken soup, undiluted
1 cup (8 ounces) sour cream
1 jar (2 ounces) pimiento, drained and diced
TOPPING:
1/2 cup butter *or* margarine, melted
1-1/3 cups finely crushed butter-flavored crackers
2 teaspoons poppy seeds

In a skillet, melt butter. Saute mushrooms until tender. Stir in chicken, soup, sour cream and pimiento; mix well. Spoon mixture into a greased 2-qt. casserole. In a small bowl, combine topping ingredients. Sprinkle over the chicken. Bake at 350° for 20 minutes. **Yield:** 6 servings

GRANDMA'S BREAKFAST FRUIT

Ethelyn Aanrud
Amherst Junction, Wisconsin

3 large cooking apples, peeled and thickly sliced
1/2 cup pitted prunes
3/4 cup raisins
1 orange, peeled and sectioned
3 cups plus 3 tablespoons water, *divided*
1/2 cup sugar
1/2 teaspoon ground cinnamon
2 tablespoons cornstarch

In a saucepan, combine apples, prunes, raisins, orange and 3 cups water. Bring to a boil; reduce heat and simmer 10 minutes. Stir in sugar and cinnamon. Combine cornstarch and remaining water; stir into saucepan. Bring to a boil, stirring constantly. Cook for 2 minutes. Chill. **Yield:** 6-8 servings. *If cooking for two:* This fruit treat keeps well in the refrigerator for a week. Enjoy on cereal or as a dessert.

BREAKFAST BUNS

Dorothy McGinnis, West Haven, Connecticut

    2 cups all-purpose flour
    3/4 cup sugar, *divided*
    1 tablespoon baking powder
    3 tablespoons butter *or*
      margarine
    2 eggs, lightly beaten
    1 teaspoon vanilla extract
    1/2 cup milk
    1 cup raisins
    1/2 teaspoon ground cinnamon

In a mixing bowl, stir together flour, 1/2 cup sugar and baking powder; cut in butter. Combine eggs, vanilla and milk; add to dry ingredients and stir just until moistened. Add raisins. Drop by tablespoonfuls onto greased baking sheet. Combine the cinnamon and remaining sugar; sprinkle over buns. Bake at 325° for 20-25 minutes or until light golden brown. Serve warm. **Yield:** 16 servings.

OVEN-ROASTED POTATOES

Margie Wampler, Butler, Pennsylvania

    2 pounds small unpeeled red
      potatoes, cut into wedges
    2 to 3 tablespoons vegetable *or*
      olive oil
    2 garlic cloves, minced
    1 tablespoon chopped fresh
      rosemary *or* 1 teaspoon dried
      rosemary
    1/2 teaspoon salt
    1/4 teaspoon pepper

Place potatoes in a 13-in. x 9-in. x 2-in. baking pan. Drizzle oil over. Sprinkle with garlic, rosemary, salt and pepper; toss gently to coat. Bake at 450° for 20-30 minutes or until potatoes are golden brown and tender when pierced with a fork. **Yield:** 6-8 servings.

HAM AND POTATOES AU GRATIN

Novella Cook, Hinton, West Virginia

    2 cups sliced peeled potatoes,
      cooked
    1 cup diced fully cooked ham
    1 tablespoon minced onion
    1/3 cup butter *or* margarine
    3 tablespoons all-purpose flour
    1-1/2 cups milk
    1 cup (4 ounces) shredded
      cheddar cheese
    3/4 teaspoon salt

Dash white pepper
Chopped fresh parsley

Combine potatoes, ham and onion in a greased 1-qt. casserole; set aside. In a saucepan, melt butter over medium heat; stir in flour until smooth. Gradually add milk, stirring constantly until mixture thickens and bubbles. Add cheese, salt and pepper; stir until cheese melts. Pour over potato mixture and stir gently to mix. Bake at 350° for 35-40 minutes or until bubbly. Garnish with parsley. **Yield:** 2 servings.

OLD-TIME POPCORN BALLS

LaReine Stevens, Ypsilanti, Michigan

    2 quarts popped popcorn
    1/2 cup molasses
    1/2 cup sugar
    1/3 cup water
    1 tablespoon vinegar
    1 tablespoon butter *or*
      margarine
    1/4 teaspoon baking soda

Place popcorn in a large bowl and set aside. In a heavy saucepan, combine molasses, sugar, water, vinegar and butter. Cook, *without stirring,* over medium heat until the mixture reaches 235° on a candy thermometer (soft-ball stage). Add baking soda and stir well. Remove from heat and immediately pour over popcorn, stirring gently with a wooden spoon until well coated. When cool enough to handle, quickly shape into 3-in. balls, dipping hands in cold water to prevent syrup from sticking. **Yield:** 6-8 servings.

LENTIL/ VEGETABLE STEW

Chris Moyers, Felton, California

    2 cups dry lentils
    3/4 cup uncooked brown rice
    1 can (28 ounces) tomatoes
      with juice, chopped
    1 can (48 ounces) tomato *or*
      vegetable juice
    4 cups water
    3 garlic cloves, minced
    1 large onion, chopped
    2 celery stalks, sliced
    3 carrots, sliced
    1 bay leaf
    1 teaspoon dried basil
    1 teaspoon dried oregano
    1 teaspoon dried thyme
    1/2 teaspoon pepper
    3 tablespoons minced fresh
      parsley

    1 zucchini, sliced
    2 medium potatoes, peeled
      and diced
    2 tablespoons lemon juice
    1 teaspoon dry mustard
Salt to taste

In a 6-qt. Dutch oven or soup kettle, combine first 15 ingredients. Bring to a boil. Reduce heat and simmer, covered, until rice and lentils are tender, 45-60 minutes. Add additional water or tomato juice if necessary. Stir in all of the remaining ingredients. Cover and continue to cook until vegetables are tender, about 45 minutes. **Yield:** 5 quarts.

CALICO PICKLES

Bob Olsen, Grand Forks, North Dakota

    4 cups sliced cucumbers
      (1-inch slices)
    2-1/4 cups sliced carrots
      (1-inch slices)
    2 cups sliced celery
      (1-inch slices)
    2 cups cubed onion
      (1-inch cubes)
    2 cups cubed sweet red pepper
      (1-inch cubes)
    1 cup cubed green pepper
      (1-inch cubes)
    1 medium head cauliflower,
      broken into florets (6 cups)
    1 cup salt
    4 quarts cold water
    2 cups sugar
    1/4 cup mustard seed
    2 tablespoons celery seed
    2 tablespoons dried whole
      black peppercorns
    1 tablespoon dried cilantro
  6-1/2 cups vinegar

Combine vegetables in a large bowl. Dissolve salt in water and pour over vegetables. Soak for 15 to 18 hours in a cool place. Drain. In a large kettle, mix sugar, spices and vinegar. Bring to a boil and boil for 3-4 minutes. Add vegetables and simmer 5-7 minutes. Pack hot into eight hot pint jars, leaving 1/4-in. headspace. Remove air bubbles. Adjust caps; process 15 minutes in boiling-water bath. **Yield:** 8 pints.

CAN'T BE BEET: Don't throw away sweet pickle juice when the pickles are all gone. Instead, pour the juice into a kettle and add a can of drained, small whole beets. Bring to a boil, then simmer for about 5 minutes. Pour into a serving dish and refrigerate. Now you've got some quickly made pickled beets.

Here are some spicy country specialties to keep your tastebuds tantalized.

Enjoy the Spiced Lemonade over ice in summer or warmed in winter for a sweet, refreshing thirst-quencher. Dig into the Chalupa Grande over crunchy corn chips, and try the Southwestern Mini Muffins by themselves or split in half and topped with thin slices of cheese or ham.

COLORFUL FARE. Clockwise from top: **Spiced Lemonade, Chalupa Grande, Southwestern Mini Muffins** (all recipes on page 79).

...fect for a blustery day, these cozy country recipes will certainly drive the chill away!

Enjoy a steaming cup or bowl of New England Fish Chowder. You'll love its creamy broth and tender chunks of potatoes. The Spanish Rice is a perfect spicy dish with your favorite roast or as a meal all by itself. And, if you're looking for a real hearty hot dish, try the Polish Poultry or the Bayou Country Seafood Casserole.

HOT IN A POT. From top to bottom: **Spanish Rice** (p. 79), **Bayou Country Seafood Casserole** (p. 79), **New England Fish Chowder** (p. 79), **Polish Poultry** (p. 80).

SPICED LEMONADE

Kim Van Rheenen, Mendota, Illinois

(PICTURED ON PAGE 77)

6 cups water, *divided*
3/4 cup sugar
2 cinnamon sticks
6 whole cloves
1 large lime, thinly sliced
1 lemon, thinly sliced
3/4 cup fresh lemon juice

In a large saucepan, bring 4 cups water, sugar, cinnamon and cloves to a boil. Reduce heat; simmer 10 minutes. Remove from heat; discard cinnamon and cloves. Cool. Pour into a large pitcher. Stir in lime, lemon, lemon juice and remaining water. Chill at least 1 hour. Can also be served warm. **Yield:** about 2 quarts.

SOUTHWESTERN MINI MUFFINS

Jennifer Dise, Phoenix, Arizona

(PICTURED ON PAGE 77)

2 cups all-purpose flour
1 tablespoon baking powder
1/2 teaspoon seasoned salt
1/4 teaspoon freshly ground black pepper
1 cup (4 ounces) shredded cheddar cheese
1 can (4 ounces) chopped green chilies, drained
1 egg, beaten
4 tablespoons Dijon mustard
1 cup milk
1/4 cup butter *or* margarine, melted

In a large bowl, combine flour, baking powder, seasoned salt and pepper. Add cheese; toss well. Stir in chilies. In a small bowl, mix egg, mustard, milk and butter. Pour over flour mixture; stir until dry ingredients are moistened. Spoon into greased mini muffin cups. Bake at 350° for 20-25 minutes or until done. Turn out onto a rack to cool. **Yield:** 36 muffins.

CHALUPA GRANDE

Cindy Bertrand, Floydada, Texas

(PICTURED ON PAGE 77)

1 pound dry pinto beans
1 pork roast (3 pounds), fat trimmed

7 cups water
1/2 cup chopped onion
2 garlic cloves, minced
2 to 3 teaspoons ground cumin
2 tablespoons chili powder
1 tablespoon salt
1 teaspoon dried oregano
1 can (4 ounces) chopped green chilies
Corn chips
Shredded cheddar cheese
Diced avocado
Diced tomatoes
Chopped green onions
Salsa

Place first 10 ingredients in a large kettle. (Beans do not need to be soaked.) Bring to a boil; reduce heat and simmer, covered, about 3 hours or until beans and roast are tender. Remove roast; cool slightly. Remove meat from bones; shred with a fork. Return meat to kettle. Cook, uncovered, until thick, about 30 minutes. Serve over corn chips. Pass remaining ingredients as toppings. **Yield:** 10-12 servings.

SPANISH RICE

Beth Wool, Barnhart, Texas

(PICTURED ON PAGE 78)

1/2 pound sliced bacon, diced
2 cans (28 ounces *each*) tomatoes with liquid, diced
1 can (10 ounces) tomatoes with green chilies with liquid, diced *or* 1 can (8 ounces) tomatoes with liquid, diced
2 cans (4 ounces *each*) chopped green chilies
1 can (8 ounces) tomato sauce
1/2 teaspoon salt
1/4 teaspoon pepper
2 cups uncooked long-grain rice

In a Dutch oven, cook bacon until crisp. Drain fat. Add all remaining ingredients. Bring mixture to a boil; reduce heat. Simmer, uncovered, over medium-low heat, until rice is tender, about 35-40 minutes. Stir occasionally to prevent scorching. **Yield:** 12-14 servings.

BAYOU COUNTRY SEAFOOD CASSEROLE

Ethel Miller, Eunice, Louisiana

(PICTURED ON PAGE 78)

6 tablespoons butter *or* margarine
1 medium onion, chopped
1 medium green pepper, chopped

1 celery stalk, chopped
1 garlic clove, minced
1 can (10-3/4 ounces) condensed cream of mushroom soup, undiluted
1 pound raw shrimp, peeled and deveined
1-1/2 cups cooked rice
2 cans (6 ounces *each*) crabmeat, drained and flaked with cartilage removed *or* 1-1/2 pounds cooked crabmeat
4 slices day-old bread, cubed
3/4 cup light cream *or* water
1/4 cup chopped green onion tops
1/2 teaspoon salt
1/4 teaspoon pepper
Dash cayenne pepper
TOPPING:
2 tablespoons butter *or* margarine, melted
1/3 cup dry bread crumbs
2 tablespoons snipped fresh parsley

In a skillet, melt butter over medium heat. Saute onion, green pepper, celery and garlic until tender. Add soup and shrimp. Cook and stir over medium heat 10 minutes or until shrimp turn pink. Stir in rice, crab, bread cubes, cream or water, onion tops and seasonings. Spoon into a greased 2-qt. baking dish. Combine topping ingredients; sprinkle over casserole. Bake at 375° for 30 minutes or until heated through. **Yield:** 8 servings.

NEW ENGLAND FISH CHOWDER

Dorothy Noonan, Quincy, Massachusetts

(PICTURED ON PAGE 78)

1/2 cup butter *or* margarine, *divided*
3 medium onions, sliced
5 medium potatoes, peeled and diced
4 teaspoons salt
1/2 teaspoon pepper
3 cups boiling water
2 pounds fresh *or* frozen haddock fillets, cut into large chunks
1 quart milk, scalded
1 can (12 ounces) evaporated milk

In a 6- to 8-qt. kettle, melt 1/4 cup butter over medium heat. Saute onions until tender but not browned. Add potatoes, salt, pepper and water. Top with fish. Simmer, covered, 25 minutes or until potatoes are fork-tender. Stir in scalded milk, evaporated milk and remaining butter; heat through. Season with additional salt and pepper if desired. **Yield:** about 4-1/2 quarts.

POLISH POULTRY

Dorothea Kampfe, Gothenburg, Nebraska

(PICTURED ON PAGE 78)

1 medium onion, chopped
1 garlic clove, minced
1 teaspoon caraway seeds
1 can (27 ounces) sauerkraut, undrained
3/4 pound smoked Polish sausage, cut into 1-inch pieces
1 broiler/fryer chicken (2 to 3 pounds), cut up
1/2 teaspoon salt
1/4 teaspoon pepper
1/4 to 1/2 teaspoon dried thyme

In a mixing bowl, combine first four ingredients. Place on the bottom of a 13-in. x 9-in. x 2-in. baking dish. Top with sausage and chicken. Sprinkle with salt, pepper and thyme. Bake at 350° for 60-65 minutes or until chicken is tender, basting occasionally with pan juices. **Yield:** 6 servings.

TALL PINES FARM SAUSAGE

Gloria Jarrett, Loveland, Ohio

2 tablespoons brown sugar
4 teaspoons salt
1 tablespoon dried sage
2 teaspoons ground savory
1 teaspoon pepper
1 teaspoon crushed dried red pepper
1/2 teaspoon ground nutmeg
2-1/2 pounds fresh ground pork*

In a large bowl, combine first seven ingredients. Mix thoroughly. Add pork; mix with hands to blend well. Cover and chill 6 hours or overnight. Shape into 12 3-1/2-in. patties. Cook patties in a skillet over medium-low heat for 10-12 minutes, turning once. Drain. (*For best results, pork should have a minimum of 15% fat.) **Yield:** 12 patties.

SAUSAGE LENTIL SOUP

Catherine Rowe, Berthoud, Colorado

1/2 pound bulk Italian sausage
1 large onion, finely chopped
1 small green pepper, finely chopped
1 small carrot, finely chopped
1 large garlic clove, finely minced
1 bay leaf

2 cans (14-1/2 ounces *each*) chicken broth
1 can (14-1/2 to 16 ounces) whole tomatoes with liquid, coarsely chopped
1 cup water
3/4 cup dry lentils
1/4 cup country-style *or* regular Dijon mustard

In a Dutch oven, brown sausage. Drain the fat and crumble sausage; return to Dutch oven along with remaining ingredients except mustard. Simmer, covered, 1 hour or until lentils and vegetables are tender. Stir in the mustard. Remove and discard bay leaf before serving. **Yield:** 6 servings.

DANISH POTATO SOUP

Sandra Halter, Akron, Ohio

1 ham bone
Water
2 potatoes, peeled and diced
6 green onions, sliced
3 celery stalks, chopped
1/4 cup minced fresh parsley
2 cups chopped cabbage
2 carrots, diced
3 tablespoons all-purpose flour
1 cup light cream
Ground nutmeg

In a soup kettle, bring ham bone and 2 quarts water to a boil. Reduce heat and simmer 1 hour or until meat pulls away from the bone. Remove ham bone. When cool enough to handle, trim any meat and dice. Discard bone. Return ham to kettle along with potatoes, onions, celery, parsley, cabbage and carrots; cook 40 minutes. Stir together flour and 1/4 cup cold water. Slowly pour into the soup, stirring constantly. Bring soup to a boil; cook 2 minutes. Reduce heat; stir in cream. Remove from the heat. Sprinkle a dash of nutmeg on each bowlful just before serving. **Yield:** 6 servings.

SOUTHERN TEA CAKES

Mary Singletary, Converse, Louisiana

1 cup shortening
1-3/4 cups sugar
2 eggs
1/2 cup milk
1/2 teaspoon vanilla extract
3 cups self-rising flour

In a mixing bowl, cream together shortening and sugar. Beat in eggs. Add milk and vanilla; beat well. Stir in flour; mix well. Drop by tablespoonsful 2-1/2-in.

apart onto greased cookie sheets. Bake at 350° for 15-20 minutes. **Yield:** about 3 dozen.

EMPIRE STATE MUFFINS

Beverly Collins, North Syracuse, New York

2 cups shredded unpeeled apples
1-1/3 cups sugar
1 cup chopped cranberries
1 cup shredded carrots
1 cup chopped walnuts *or* pecans
2-1/2 cups all-purpose flour
1 tablespoon baking powder
2 teaspoons baking soda
1/2 teaspoon salt
2 teaspoons ground cinnamon
2 eggs, lightly beaten
1/2 cup vegetable oil

In a large mixing bowl, combine apples and sugar. Gently fold in cranberries, carrots and nuts. Combine dry ingredients; add to mixing bowl. Mix well to moisten dry ingredients. Combine eggs and oil; stir into apple mixture. Fill 18 greased muffin tins 2/3 full. Bake at 375° for 20-25 minutes. Cool 5 minutes before removing from tins. **Yield:** 18 muffins.

SWEET POTATO SALAD

Lettie Baker, Pennsboro, West Virginia

✓ This tasty dish uses less sugar, salt and fat. Recipe includes *Diabetic Exchanges*.

3 pounds sweet potatoes, cooked, peeled and cubed
1/2 cup finely chopped onion
1 cup chopped green pepper
1-1/2 teaspoons salt, optional
1/4 teaspoon pepper
1-1/2 cups light *or* regular mayonnaise
Dash hot pepper sauce

Combine first five ingredients in a large bowl. Stir in mayonnaise and hot pepper sauce; mix well. Cover and refrigerate at least 1 hour before serving. **Yield:** 10 servings. **Diabetic Exchanges:** One serving (with no added salt and using light mayonnaise) equals 2 starch, 1-1/2 fat; also, 217 calories, 167 mg sodium, 5 mg cholesterol, 38 gm carbohydrate, 4 gm protein, 7 gm fat.

CHILI CHEESE DIP
Jerrie West, Oakhurst, California

1 can (15 ounces) chili con carne without beans
1 pound process American cheese, cubed
1 can (4 ounces) chopped green chilies
Tortilla chips

Combine chili, cheese and green chilies in a saucepan or fondue pot. Heat over medium-low, stirring frequently, until the cheese melts. Serve warm with tortilla chips. **Yield:** 12 servings.

MAPLE SUGAR PUMPKIN PIE
Martha Boudah, Essex Center, Vermont

1 can (16 ounces) solid-pack pumpkin
2 tablespoons all-purpose flour
1/2 teaspoon ground cinnamon
1/2 teaspoon ground nutmeg
1/2 teaspoon ground ginger
1 tablespoon butter *or* margarine, softened
1 cup sugar
1 cup milk
2 tablespoons maple syrup
2 eggs
1 unbaked pie shell (9 inches)
Whipped cream, optional

In a mixing bowl, combine all ingredients except last two. Pour into the pie shell. Bake at 425° for 15 minutes. Reduce heat to 350° and continue baking for about 45 minutes or until a knife inserted near the center comes out clean. Cool to room temperature. Refrigerate. Garnish with whipped cream if desired. **Yield:** 8 servings.

CHOCOLATE COCONUT CREAM PIE
Nancy Reichert, Thomasville, Georgia

1 unbaked pie pastry (9 inches)
2/3 cup sugar
1/3 cup cornstarch
1/4 teaspoon salt
3 cups milk
3 egg yolks
1 tablespoon butter *or* margarine
2 teaspoons vanilla extract
1/2 cup flaked coconut

CHOCOLATE LAYER:
3 tablespoons unsweetened cocoa
3 tablespoons sugar
2 tablespoons milk
MERINGUE:
3 egg whites
1/4 teaspoon cream of tartar
6 tablespoons sugar

Bake pie pastry. Cool. Meanwhile, in a saucepan, combine sugar, cornstarch and salt; stir in milk. Cook and stir over medium-high heat until thickened and bubbly. Reduce heat; cook and stir 2 minutes more. Remove from the heat. Beat egg yolks lightly. Stir a little of the hot mixture into the yolks; return all to saucepan. Bring to a gentle boil. Cook and stir 2 minutes more. Remove from the heat. Stir in butter and vanilla. Pour 1-1/2 cups mixture into small bowl; add coconut to bowl and set aside. Combine chocolate layer ingredients; blend into remaining mixture in saucepan. Return to heat; cook and stir until mixture begins to boil. Remove from the heat; spread 1 cup over bottom of pie crust. Top with coconut mixture and finish with remaining chocolate mixture. For meringue, beat egg whites with cream of tartar until foamy. Gradually add sugar, beating until stiff peaks form. Spread over hot filling, sealing to edges of pie crust. Bake at 350° for 12-15 minutes or until lightly browned. Cool to room temperature; chill several hours before serving. **Yield:** 8 servings.

PLANTATION STUFFED PEPPERS
Sherry Morgan, Mansfield, Louisiana

8 medium green peppers, tops and seeds removed
1 pound ground beef
1 cup chopped onion
1 garlic clove, minced
2 teaspoons chili powder
1 teaspoon salt
1/2 teaspoon pepper
2 cans (10-3/4 ounces *each*) tomato soup, undiluted
2 cups (8 ounces) shredded cheddar cheese
1-1/2 cups cooked rice

In boiling salted water, cook peppers for 3-5 minutes. Remove and set aside. In a skillet, cook beef, onion and garlic until meat is done and onion is tender. Drain any fat. Add seasonings and soup; simmer, uncovered, for 10 minutes. Stir in cheese; cook and stir until melted. Stir in rice. Fill peppers; place in a shallow baking dish. Bake at 350° for 20 minutes. **Yield:** 8 servings.

ZUCCHINI COLESLAW
Aloma Hawkins, Bixby, Missouri

☑ This tasty dish uses less sugar, salt and fat. Recipe includes *Diabetic Exchanges*.

2 cups coarsely shredded zucchini
2 cups shredded cabbage
1 medium carrot, shredded
2 green onions, sliced
1/2 cup thinly sliced radishes
1/3 cup light mayonnaise
1/3 cup mild picante sauce
1/2 teaspoon ground cumin

Drain zucchini by pressing between layers of paper towels. Place in a large bowl and combine with cabbage, carrot, onions and radishes. In a small bowl, combine remaining ingredients. Pour over vegetables and toss well. Cover and chill at least 1 hour. **Yield:** 8 servings. **Diabetic Exchanges:** One serving equals 1 vegetable, 1/2 fat; also, 55 calories, 154 mg sodium, 2 mg cholesterol, 7 gm carbohydrate, 1 gm protein, 3 gm fat.

FRESH RASPBERRY PIE
Deanna Richter, Elmore, Minnesota

CRUST:
1-1/2 cups graham cracker crumbs (about 20 squares)
3 tablespoons sugar
1/3 cup butter *or* margarine, melted
FILLING:
24 large marshmallows
1/3 cup milk
2/3 cup whipping cream, whipped
Few drops red food coloring, optional
2 cups fresh raspberries, *divided*

Combine crust ingredients. Press into a 9-in. pie plate; chill. Meanwhile, heat marshmallows and milk in a saucepan over low until smooth. Cool. Fold in cream, and food coloring if desired. Spoon half into the crust. Top with half the raspberries. Repeat layers. Chill until firm, about 3 hours. **Yield:** 8 servings.

FOOLPROOF PIE CRUSTS: Making pie crust is easier if you chill all the ingredients before making the dough. Mix the flour, salt and shortening ahead and store in the refrigerator. When it's time to prepare your pie, add ice water to make dough. Cover and chill the dough for 30 minutes or longer before rolling out.

81

FALAFALAS

Jodi Sykes, Lake Worth, Florida

2 cans (15 ounces *each*)
   garbanzo beans, rinsed and
   drained
2 green onions, minced
1 cup fresh bean sprouts
1/4 cup hulled sunflower seeds
1/4 cup dry bread crumbs
1 egg
1/2 teaspoon garlic powder
1/4 teaspoon salt
1/4 teaspoon pepper
2 tablespoons soy sauce
2 tablespoons Worcestershire
   sauce
2 tablespoons cooking oil
YOGURT SAUCE:
2 cups (16 ounces) plain yogurt
1 green onion, minced
1 tablespoon fresh dill weed
1 garlic clove, minced

9 pita bread halves
1 tomato, sliced
1 red onion, sliced
Lettuce leaves

In a food processor, combine first 11 ingredients. Process until smooth and well mixed. If mixture is moist, add a few more bread crumbs. Using a 1/3 cup measure, shape mixture into patties. In a skillet, heat oil over medium-high. Fry patties until golden brown on both sides. Meanwhile, combine sauce ingredients. Stuff pita halves with patties, tomato, onion and lettuce. Spoon sauce into pitas. Serve immediately. **Yield:** 9 servings.

OLD SETTLERS' BAKED BEANS

Kathy Schulz, Sand Springs, Oklahoma

1/2 pound ground beef
1/2 pound bacon, diced
1 medium onion, chopped
1/3 cup sugar
1/3 cup packed brown sugar
1/4 cup ketchup
1/4 cup barbecue sauce
1 tablespoon prepared mustard
1/2 teaspoon pepper
1/2 teaspoon chili powder
1 can (16 ounces) pork and
   beans, undrained
1 can (16 ounces) kidney
   beans, rinsed and drained
1 can (16 ounces) great
   northern beans, rinsed and
   drained

In a large skillet, cook beef, bacon and onion until meat is done and onion is tender. Drain any fat. Combine all remaining ingredients except beans. Add to meat mixture; mix well. Stir in beans. Place in a greased 2-1/2-qt. casserole. Bake, covered, at 350° for 1 hour or until heated through. **Yield:** 8-10 servings.

GRILLED FLANK STEAK

Jenny Reece, Farwell, Minnesota

✓ This tasty dish uses less sugar, salt and fat. Recipe includes *Diabetic Exchanges*.

1/4 cup soy sauce
2 tablespoons vinegar
1 green onion, sliced
1-1/2 teaspoons garlic powder
1-1/2 teaspoons ground ginger
3 tablespoons honey
3/4 cup vegetable oil
1 beef flank steak (about 1-1/2
   pounds)
1 pound fresh mushrooms,
   sliced
1 green pepper, cut into thin
   strips
1 yellow *or* sweet red pepper,
   cut into thin strips
3 carrots, cut into julienne strips

In a glass baking dish, combine first seven ingredients. Place meat in marinade; cover and refrigerate for 24 hours, turning once. Remove meat and reserve marinade. Grill meat over hot coals until cooked to your preference (about 15 minutes for medium). Meanwhile, in a skillet, saute vegetables in 1/4 cup marinade until tender. Slice meat at an angle into thin strips and serve with vegetables. **Yield:** 5 servings. **Diabetic Exchanges:** One serving equals 3 lean meat, 2 vegetable, 1 fat; also, 265 calories, 173 mg sodium, 65 mg cholesterol, 11 gm carbohydrate, 28 gm protein, 12 gm fat.

ZUCCHINI QUICHE

Dorothy Collins, Winnsboro, Texas

1 unbaked pie pastry (9 inches)
2 tablespoons butter *or*
   margarine
1 pound zucchini, thinly sliced
1-1/2 cups (6 ounces) shredded
   mozzarella cheese
1 cup ricotta cheese *or* dry
   cottage cheese
1/2 cup half-and-half cream
3 eggs, lightly beaten
3/4 teaspoon salt
1/2 teaspoon dried oregano
1/2 teaspoon dried basil

1/4 teaspoon garlic powder
Dash pepper
Paprika

Prick bottom of pie crust with a fork and bake at 425° for 7 minutes. Remove crust from oven; set aside. Reduce heat to 350°. In a skillet, melt butter over medium-high heat; saute zucchini until tender. Drain. Place half the zucchini in the bottom of the crust. Sprinkle with mozzarella cheese. In a bowl, combine ricotta or cottage cheese, cream, eggs, salt, oregano, basil, garlic powder and pepper. Pour into crust. Arrange the remaining zucchini slices on top. Sprinkle with paprika. Bake about 45 minutes or until a knife inserted in the center comes out clean. **Yield:** 6-8 servings.

MOLDED LIME SALAD

Jean Parsons, Sarver, Pennsylvania

2 cups boiling water
1 package (6 ounces) lime-
   flavored gelatin
1 cup cold water
1 tablespoon vinegar
Dash salt
Dash white pepper, optional
3/4 cup mayonnaise
1/2 cup shredded carrots
1/2 cup finely chopped peeled
   cucumber
1/2 cup finely chopped celery
1/2 cup finely chopped green
   pepper
2 tablespoons finely chopped
   onion
Carrot curls, optional

In a mixing bowl, pour boiling water over gelatin. Stir to dissolve. Add cold water, vinegar, salt, and pepper if desired. Pour 1 cup of mixture into a 6-cup mold; set aside. Chill remaining gelatin for 30 minutes, then add mayonnaise and blend with a rotary beater until smooth. Chill until almost set. Meanwhile, chill gelatin in mold until almost set. Turn mayonnaise/gelatin mixture into a bowl and whip until fluffy. Fold in vegetables. Spoon into mold. Chill until firm. Unmold to serve. Garnish with carrot curls if desired. **Yield:** 8-10 servings.

HOLD IT! Here's an idea for holding recipe cards while you're cooking. Place a card between the tongs of a fork and put the fork upside down in an empty glass. This holds the card at the right angle to read and also keeps it off the counter and out of the way of spatters and spills.

MEALS IN MINUTES

EVEN in sunny Arizona, the pace slows somewhat during winter, permitting busy cooks a bit more time to prepare elaborate meals.

Still, there are days when minutes matter at mealtime. When they do, Michel Karkula of Chandler is all set to serve up a satisfying spread!

"Years ago, I relied on recipes I could fix fast for my growing family," she relates. "Today, when the children and grandchildren come to visit, I still use some of them."

One such "old friend" in Michel's kitchen is hearty Posse Stew, which can be called into action in a hurry from the pantry and easily expanded.

Also finished in minutes are spicy, moist Pumpkin Muffins. They can be prepared with little fuss from a biscuit mix, canned pumpkin and spices.

For dessert, Michel's tapioca and banana pudding—served either warm or cold—brims with old-fashioned taste (make it ahead, if you like).

Next time *you* have one of those "need-to-feed-'em-fast" days, turn to Michel's menu for the solution. Your family will be quick to thank you!

POSSE STEW

- 1 pound ground beef *or* turkey
- 1 medium onion, diced
- 1 can (16 ounces) tomatoes, undrained
- 1 can (15 ounces) chili beans, undrained
- 1 can (4 ounces) diced green chilies, undrained
- 1 can (15-1/2 ounces) hominy, drained
- 1 can (16 ounces) whole

kernel corn, drained
Salt and pepper to taste
- 1 tablespoon cornstarch, optional
- 1/4 cup water, optional

In a skillet, brown ground meat and onion; drain. Stir in tomatoes, beans, chilies, hominy and corn; season with salt and pepper. For a thicker stew, combine cornstarch and water, then stir into stew. Cook and stir until thickened. **Yield:** 4-6 servings.

PUMPKIN SPICE MUFFINS

- 1/2 cup canned pumpkin
- 1/2 cup milk
- 1 egg
- 2 cups biscuit mix
- 1/4 cup sugar
- 1/2 teaspoon ground nutmeg
- 1/2 teaspoon ground cinnamon
- 1/2 teaspoon ground ginger
STREUSEL TOPPING:
- 1 tablespoon biscuit mix
- 2 tablespoons sugar
- 1/4 teaspoon ground cinnamon
- 2 teaspoons butter *or* margarine, softened

In a mixing bowl, combine pumpkin, milk and egg with a fork. Combine dry ingredients; add to mixing bowl and stir just until moistened. Spoon into 12 well-greased muffin cups. Combine streusel ingredients; sprinkle over

muffins. Bake at 400° for 15 minutes or until golden brown. Serve warm. **Yield:** 1 dozen.

BANANA TAPIOCA PUDDING

- 2-3/4 cups milk
- 3 tablespoons quick-cooking tapioca
- 1/3 cup sugar
- 1 egg, lightly beaten
- 1 teaspoon vanilla extract
- 2 bananas, sliced

In a saucepan, combine milk, tapioca, sugar and egg; let stand 5 minutes. Cook and stir over medium heat until mixture comes to a full boil; remove from heat. Stir in vanilla and bananas. Cool for 20 minutes. Serve warm or cold. **Yield:** 6 servings.

TASTY GROUND TURKEY: Fresh, uncooked ground turkey makes an interesting substitute for ground beef in dishes like the Posse Stew on this page. Also try ground turkey for Stroganoff, "Sloppy Toms", spaghetti sauce, lasagna, tacos, enchiladas, casseroles and as all or part of the meat in meat loaf. Season sparingly, since ground turkey does accept seasoning more readily than do other ground meats.

THE HOLIDAYS can be hectic—so here's a baker's half-dozen of ways to fill the cookie jar fast!

LEMON SNOWFLAKES

Linda Barry, Dianna, Texas

1 package (18-1/4 ounces) lemon cake mix with pudding
2-1/4 cups frozen whipped topping, thawed
1 egg
Confectioners' sugar

In a mixing bowl, combine cake mix, whipped topping and egg. Beat with electric mixer on medium speed until blended. Batter will be very sticky. Drop by teaspoonful into confectioners' sugar; roll lightly to coat. Place on ungreased cookie sheets. Bake at 350° for 10-12 minutes or until lightly brown. **Yield:** 5-6 dozen.

CRISP BUTTER COOKIES

Tammy Mackie, Seward, Nebraska

1/2 cup butter *or* margarine, softened
1 cup sugar
5 egg yolks
2 cups all-purpose flour
Colored sugar

In a mixing bowl, cream butter and sugar. Blend in egg yolks. Add flour, 1 cup at a time, beating well after each addition. Dough will be very stiff. On a well-floured board or pastry cloth, roll

YOU'LL be out of the kitchen quick when you bake Crisp Butter Cookies, Lemon Snowflakes.

out dough to a 1/8-in. thickness. Using a pastry wheel or knife, cut into 2-1/2-in. squares, rectangles or diamonds. Place 1/2 in. apart on ungreased cookie sheets. Sprinkle with colored sugar. Bake at 375° for 7-8 minutes or until lightly browned. **Yield:** 6 dozen.

DATE DELIGHTS

Helen Wolber, Brookville, Indiana

1 cup sugar
1/2 cup butter *or* margarine
1 egg
3/4 cup chopped dates
3/4 cup chopped pecans
2 cups crisp rice cereal
Confectioners' sugar

Combine sugar, butter, egg, dates and pecans in a heavy saucepan; bring to a boil, stirring thoroughly. Cook over medium heat until well blended, about 5 minutes. Remove from heat and stir in cereal. Cool. With buttered hands, roll into 1-in. balls; roll in confectioners' sugar. **Yield:** about 4 dozen.

HOLIDAY MACAROONS

Kristine Conway, Mogadore, Ohio

4 eggs
1-1/2 cups sugar
2/3 cup all-purpose flour
1/2 teaspoon baking powder
1/4 teaspoon salt
2 tablespoons butter *or* margarine, melted and cooled
1 teaspoon vanilla extract
5 cups flaked coconut
1 jar (10 ounces) maraschino cherries, drained and halved

In a mixing bowl, beat the eggs until foamy. Gradually add sugar, beating constantly until thick and pale yellow. Stir together dry ingredients; fold into egg mixture. Stir in butter, vanilla and coconut. Drop by teaspoonfuls onto greased and floured cookie sheets. Top with cherries. Bake at 325° for 10-13 minutes. **Yield:** about 6 dozen.

FRUITCAKE SQUARES

Lana Rulevish, Ashley, Illinois

6 tablespoons butter *or* margarine, melted
4 cups vanilla wafer crumbs

3/4 cup halved candied green cherries
3/4 cup halved candied red cherries
1/2 cup chopped candied pineapple
3/4 cup chopped dates
1 cup pecan halves
1 can (14 ounces) sweetened condensed milk
1 teaspoon vanilla extract

Pour melted butter in a 15-in. x 10-in. x 1-in. baking pan. Sprinkle evenly with vanilla wafer crumbs. Arrange cherries, pineapple, dates and pecans evenly over the crumbs; press down gently. Combine milk and vanilla; pour over fruit. Bake at 350° for 20-25 minutes. **Yield:** about 6 dozen.

PEPPERMINT COOKIES

Donna Lock, Fort Collins, Colorado

2/3 cup butter-flavored shortening
1/4 cup sugar
1/4 cup packed brown sugar
1 egg
1-1/2 cups all-purpose flour
1/2 teaspoon baking powder
1/2 teaspoon salt
1/2 cup crushed peppermint candy

In a mixing bowl, cream shortening and sugars; beat in egg. Combine flour, baking powder and salt; stir into the creamed mixture. Fold in the candy. Drop by teaspoonsful onto a greased cookie sheet. Bake at 350° for 10-12 minutes or until cookie edges just begin to brown. **Yield:** 3-1/2 dozen.

CHOCOLATE CLUSTERS

Sara Ann Fowler, Illinois City, Illinois

2 pounds white chocolate *or* almond bark
1 cup creamy *or* chunky peanut butter
2 cups salted dry roasted peanuts
3 cups pastel miniature marshmallows
4 cups crisp rice cereal

Melt white chocolate and peanut butter in microwave or double boiler, stirring often to mix well. Add all remaining ingredients; stir with wooden spoon to coat evenly. Drop by teaspoonsful onto waxed paper. **Yield:** 11 dozen.

Sparkling Almond Raspberry Stars, rich Fudge Puddles, buttery Whipped Shortbread, colorful Rainbow Cookies. No matter what the shape or flavor, there's something special about baking, decorating and giving cookies at Christmas. Below and on the next two pages, you'll sample the favorites of a dozen country cooks.

SEASON'S EATINGS! Clockwise from top: **Almond Raspberry Stars, Fudge Puddles, Whipped Shortbread, Rainbow Cookies** (all recipes on page 89).

Mix up a batch of memories for Christmas! Children will love to help with Molasses Spice Cutouts and Vanilla-Butter Sugar Cookies. Keep a plate of cheery Holly Wreaths on hand for neighbors who drop by. Don't forget to leave an assortment for Santa to enjoy on Christmas Eve! In all their many shapes and flavors, home-baked cookies come from the heart.

SWEET TREATS. Clockwise from lower left: **Finnish Pinwheels** (p. 90), **Molasses Spice Cutouts** (p. 90), **Eggnog Logs** (p. 90), **Italian Sprinkle Cookies** (p. 90), **Cherry Mocha Balls** (p. 91), **Vanilla-Butter Sugar Cookies** (p. 91), **Miniature Christmas Fruitcakes** (p. 91), **Holly Wreaths** (p. 91).

ompany's coming! Here's a perfect meal for holiday get-togethers with family and friends. Frozen Cranberry Salad is a cool and tangy complement to Cornish Hens with Wild Rice. Top off the meal with Maple-Glazed Apple Pie, a spicy twist on a down-home favorite.

HOME FOR THE HOLIDAYS. Clockwise from top right: **Maple-Glazed Apple Pie** (p. 91), **Cornish Hens with Wild Rice** (p. 92), **Frozen Cranberry Salad** (p. 92).

RAINBOW COOKIES

Mary Ann Lee, Marco Island, Florida

(PICTURED ON PAGE 85)

1 can (8 ounces) almond paste
1 cup butter, softened (no substitutes)
1 cup sugar
4 eggs, *separated*
2 cups all-purpose flour
6 to 8 drops red food coloring
6 to 8 drops green food coloring
1/4 cup seedless red raspberry jam
1/4 cup apricot jam
1 cup (6 ounces) semisweet chocolate chips

Grease the bottoms of three matching 13-in. x 9-in. x 2-in. baking pans (or re-use one pan). Line the pans with waxed paper; grease the paper. Place almond paste in a large mixing bowl; break up with a fork. Cream with butter, sugar and egg yolks until light, fluffy and smooth. Stir in flour. In another mixing bowl, beat egg whites until soft peaks form. Fold into dough, mixing until thoroughly blended. Divide dough into three portions (about 1-1/3 cups each). Color one portion with red food coloring and one with green; leave the remaining portion uncolored. Spread each portion into the prepared pans. Bake at 350° for 10-12 minutes or until edges are light golden brown. Invert onto wire racks; remove waxed paper. Place another wire rack on top and turn over. Cool completely. Place green layer on a large piece of plastic wrap. Spread evenly with raspberry jam. Top with uncolored layer and spread with apricot jam. Top with pink layer. Bring plastic wrap over layers. Slide onto a cookie sheet and set a cutting board or heavy, flat pan on top to compress layers. Refrigerate overnight. The next day, melt chocolate in a double boiler. Spread over top layer; allow to harden. With a sharp knife, trim edges. Cut into 1/2-in. strips across the width; then cut each strip into 4-5 pieces. Store in airtight containers. **Yield:** about 8 dozen.

ALMOND RASPBERRY STARS

Darlene Weaver, Lebanon, Pennsylvania

(PICTURED ON PAGE 85)

3/4 cup butter *or* margarine
1/2 cup confectioners' sugar
1 teaspoon vanilla extract
1/2 teaspoon almond extract
1-3/4 cups plus 2 tablespoons all-purpose flour
2 tablespoons finely chopped almonds
1 tablespoon sugar
1/2 teaspoon ground cinnamon
1 egg white, lightly beaten
1/3 cup raspberry jam

In a mixing bowl, cream the butter and confectioners' sugar until light and fluffy. Add extracts and beat until well mixed. Stir in flour. Shape into a ball; cover and chill for 15 minutes. On a lightly floured board, roll dough to a 1/4-in. thickness. Cut into about 72 stars, half 2-1/2 in. and half 1-1/2 in. Combine almonds, sugar and cinnamon. Brush small stars with egg white and immediately sprinkle with cinnamon/sugar mixture. Leave large stars plain. Bake on ungreased cookie sheets at 350° for 10 minutes (small stars) to 12 minutes (large stars) or until the tips just begin to brown. Cool on wire racks. To assemble, spread enough jam over large star to cover the center. Top with a small star. Press lightly; jam should show around edge of small star. Let jam set before storing. **Yield:** about 3 dozen.

FUDGE PUDDLES

Kimarie Maassen, Avoca, Iowa

(PICTURED ON PAGE 85)

1/2 cup butter *or* margarine, softened
1/2 cup creamy peanut butter
1/2 cup sugar
1/2 cup packed light brown sugar
1 egg
1/2 teaspoon vanilla extract
1-1/4 cups all-purpose flour
3/4 teaspoon baking soda
1/2 teaspoon salt
FUDGE FILLING:
1 cup (6 ounces) milk chocolate chips
1 cup (6 ounces) semisweet chocolate chips
1 can (14 ounces) sweetened condensed milk
1 teaspoon vanilla extract
Chopped peanuts

In a mixing bowl, cream butter, peanut butter and sugars; add egg and vanilla. Stir together flour, baking soda and salt; add to creamed mixture. Mix well. Chill for 1 hour. Shape into 48 balls, 1 in. each. Place in lightly greased mini-muffin tins. Bake at 325° for 14-16 minutes or until lightly browned. Remove from oven and immediately make "wells" in the center of each by lightly pressing with a melon baller. Cool in pans for 5 minutes, then carefully remove to wire racks. For filling, melt chocolate chips in a double boiler over simmering water. Stir in milk and vanilla; mix well. Using a small pitcher or pastry bag, fill each shell with filling. Sprinkle with peanuts. (Leftover filling can be stored in the refrigerator and served warm over ice cream.) **Yield:** 4 dozen.

WHIPPED SHORTBREAD

Jane Ficiur, Bow Island, Alberta

(PICTURED ON PAGE 85)

3 cups butter, softened (no substitutes)
1-1/2 cups confectioners' sugar, sifted
4-1/2 cups all-purpose flour
1-1/2 cups cornstarch
Nonpareils *and/or* halved candied cherries

Using a heavy-duty mixer, beat butter on medium speed until light and fluffy. Gradually add dry ingredients, beating constantly until well blended. Dust hands lightly with additional cornstarch. Roll dough into 1-in. balls, dip in nonpareils and place on ungreased cookie sheet. Press lightly with a floured fork. To decorate with cherries, place balls on cookie sheet and press lightly with fork. Top each with a cherry half. Bake at 300° for 20-22 minutes or until cookie is set but not browned. **Yield:** 16-18 dozen. *Editor's note:* Yes, this recipe does call for 1-1/2 cups cornstarch.

PEPPERY SNAPS

Joan Elbourn, Gardner, Massachusetts

1-1/4 cups all-purpose flour
1 cup whole wheat flour
1-1/2 teaspoons baking soda
1 teaspoon ground anise seed
1/2 teaspoon salt
1/2 teaspoon ground ginger
1/4 teaspoon pepper
1 cup packed light brown sugar
3 tablespoons light molasses
3/4 cup butter *or* margarine, softened
1 egg
Sugar

Combine first seven ingredients; set aside. In a mixing bowl, beat brown sugar, molasses, butter and egg. Stir in dry ingredients; mix well. Chill for 1 hour. Shape into 1-in. balls. Roll in sugar and place on ungreased cookie sheets. Bake at 350° for 10-13 minutes. Cool cookies about 1 minute before removing to wire racks. **Yield:** 6-7 dozen.

FINNISH PINWHEELS
Ilona Barron, Ontonagon, Michigan

(PICTURED ON PAGE 86)

FILLING:
 1/2 pound pitted prunes, chopped
 1/2 pound pitted dates, chopped
 1 cup boiling water
 2 tablespoons sugar
 1 tablespoon butter *or*
 margarine
PASTRY:
 3 cups all-purpose flour
 1 cup sugar
 2 teaspoons baking powder
 1/2 teaspoon salt
 1 cup butter
 1 egg, beaten
 3 tablespoons cream
 1 teaspoon vanilla extract
Confectioners' sugar, optional

In a saucepan, combine prunes, dates, water and sugar. Cook over low heat, stirring constantly, until thickened. Remove from the heat and stir in butter. Cool. Meanwhile, in a mixing bowl, sift together flour, sugar, baking powder and salt. Cut in butter as for a pie pastry. Blend in egg, cream and vanilla. Form into two balls. Place one ball at a time on a floured board and roll to a 1/8-in. thickness. Cut into 2-in. squares. Place on ungreased cookie sheets. Make 1-in. slits in corners (Fig. 1). Place 1/2 teaspoon filling in the center of each square. Bring every other corner up into center to form a pinwheel and press lightly (Fig. 2). Repeat with remaining dough and filling. Bake at 325° for 12 minutes or until the points are light golden brown. Sprinkle with confectioners' sugar if desired. **Yield:** about 7 dozen.

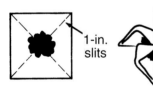

Fig. 1   1-in. slits   Fig. 2

MOLASSES SPICE CUTOUTS
Doris Heinen, St. Cloud, Minnesota

(PICTURED ON PAGE 86)

 1 cup butter *or* margarine,
 softened
 1-1/2 cups sugar
 1 cup light molasses
 1/2 cup cold coffee
 6 cups all-purpose flour
 2 teaspoons baking soda
 1 teaspoon salt
 1/2 teaspoon ground nutmeg
 1/4 teaspoon ground cloves
ICING (optional):
 1 envelope unflavored gelatin
 3/4 cup cold water
 3/4 cup sugar
 3/4 cup confectioners' sugar
 3/4 teaspoon baking powder
 1/2 teaspoon vanilla extract
Colored sugar *or* nonpareils

Decorator icing, optional

In a mixing bowl, cream butter and sugar; beat in molasses and coffee. Stir together flour, baking soda, salt and spices; add to molasses mixture and mix well. Chill dough 1-2 hours or until easy to handle. If needed, add a little additional flour before rolling. On a lightly floured surface, roll dough to a 1/4-in. thickness. Cut with holiday cutters dipped in flour. Place on ungreased baking sheets. Bake at 350° for 12-15 minutes. Cool on wire racks. For icing, if desired, combine gelatin and water in a small saucepan. Let stand for 5 minutes to soften. Add sugar. Heat and stir over very low heat until the gelatin and sugar dissolve. Transfer to a mixing bowl. Add confectioners' sugar; beat until foamy. Add baking powder and vanilla; beat until very thick, about 10 minutes. Frost cookies by inverting them and quickly swirling the tops in the icing; decorate with colored sugar or nonpareils. For traditional gingerbread men, use decorator icing to add features as desired. **Yield:** about 7-8 dozen (2-1/2-in. cookies).

EGGNOG LOGS
Kim Jordan, Dunsmuir, California

(PICTURED ON PAGE 86)

 1 cup butter *or* margarine,
 softened
 3/4 cup sugar
 1-1/4 teaspoons ground nutmeg
 1 egg
 2 teaspoons vanilla extract
 1/2 to 1 teaspoon rum extract
 3 cups all-purpose flour
FROSTING:
 1/4 cup butter *or* margarine,
 softened
 3 cups confectioners' sugar,
 divided
 1 teaspoon vanilla extract
 1/2 to 1 teaspoon rum extract
 2 tablespoons light cream
Ground nutmeg

In a mixing bowl, cream butter and sugar. Add the nutmeg, egg and extracts; mix thoroughly. Stir in flour. If necessary, chill dough for easier handling. On a lightly floured surface, shape dough into 1/2-in.-diameter rolls; cut

each into 3-in.-long pieces. Place 2 in. apart on ungreased baking sheets. Bake at 350° for 15 minutes or until lightly browned. Cool on wire racks. For frosting, cream butter until light and fluffy. Add 2 cups sugar and extracts; mix well. Beat in cream and remaining sugar. Frost cookies. With tines of a small fork, make lines down the frosting to simulate bark. Sprinkle with nutmeg. **Yield:** 4-1/2 dozen.

ITALIAN SPRINKLE COOKIES
Gloria Cracchiolo, Newburgh, New York

(PICTURED ON PAGE 87)

 6 eggs
 5 cups all-purpose flour
 2 cups confectioners' sugar
 2 tablespoons plus 1-1/2
 teaspoons baking powder
 1 cup shortening, melted
 1 tablespoon almond extract
 1-1/2 teaspoons lemon extract
GLAZE:
 1/2 cup warm milk
 1 teaspoon almond extract
 1 teaspoon vanilla extract
 1 box (1 pound) confectioners'
 sugar
Colored sprinkles (jimmies)

Using a heavy-duty electric mixer on high speed, beat eggs until light and foamy, about 5 minutes. Set aside. In another mixing bowl, stir together flour, sugar and baking powder; gradually add shortening and extracts until a bead-like texture is formed. Gradually add beaten eggs (dough will be stiff). Roll dough into 1-in. balls. Place on ungreased baking sheets. Bake at 350° for 12 minutes. The tops of the cookies will not brown, but the bottoms should brown slightly. For glaze, combine milk and extracts in a large bowl. Add sugar; whisk until all lumps are dissolved and the glaze is smooth. As soon as cookies are removed from the oven, quickly immerse two or three at a time into the glaze. Remove with a slotted spoon or fingers. Place cookies on wire racks to drain. Quickly top with sprinkles. Let dry 24 hours before storing in airtight containers. **Yield:** about 7 dozen.

BETTER BUTTER: Some cookie recipes call for using butter only—not butter *or* margarine, as ordinarily. For best results with these recipes, don't substitute—even with a "light" butter product. (They can contain added water and may not work correctly.)

CHERRY MOCHA BALLS

Jeana Crowell, Whitewater, Kansas

(PICTURED ON PAGE 87)

1 cup butter, softened
1/2 cup sugar
4 teaspoons vanilla extract
2 cups all-purpose flour
1/4 cup unsweetened cocoa
1 tablespoon instant coffee granules
1/2 teaspoon salt
1 cup finely chopped pecans
2/3 cup chopped red candied cherries
Confectioners' sugar

In a mixing bowl, cream butter. Gradually add sugar and vanilla; beat until light and fluffy. Stir together flour, cocoa, coffee and salt; gradually add to creamed mixture. Mix well. Stir in pecans and cherries. Chill dough for ease of handling if necessary. Shape into 1-in. balls and place on ungreased cookie sheets. Bake at 350° for 15 minutes or until cookies are set. Cool on wire racks. Dust with confectioners' sugar. **Yield:** about 6 dozen.

VANILLA-BUTTER SUGAR COOKIES

Cindy Ettel, Hutchinson, Minnesota

(PICTURED ON PAGE 87)

1-1/2 cups sugar
1-1/2 cups butter, softened (no substitutes)
2 eggs
2 tablespoons vanilla extract
4 cups all-purpose flour
1 teaspoon salt
1 teaspoon baking soda
1 teaspoon cream of tartar
FROSTING:
1-1/2 cups confectioners' sugar
3 tablespoons butter, softened
1 tablespoon vanilla extract
1 tablespoon milk
Food coloring, optional
Colored sugar

In a mixing bowl, combine sugar and butter; beat until creamy. Add eggs and vanilla; beat well. Stir together dry ingredients; gradually add to creamed mixture until completely blended. Chill for 30 minutes. On a lightly floured surface, roll dough to a 1/4-in. thickness. Cut with holiday cutters dipped in flour. Using a floured spatula, transfer cookies to ungreased baking sheets. Bake at 350° for 10-12 minutes. Cool on wire racks. For frosting, combine sugar, butter, vanilla and milk; beat until creamy. Thin with additional milk to desired spreading consistency if necessary. Add a few drops of food coloring if desired. Spread frosting over cookies and decorate with colored sugar. **Yield:** 7 dozen (2-1/2-in. cookies).

MINIATURE CHRISTMAS FRUITCAKES

Libby Over, Phillipsburg, Ohio

(PICTURED ON PAGE 87)

1/2 cup light molasses
1/4 cup water
1 teaspoon vanilla extract
1 box (15 ounces) raisins
1 pound candied fruit, chopped
1/2 cup butter *or* margarine
2/3 cup sugar
3 eggs
1 cup plus 2 tablespoons all-purpose flour
1/4 teaspoon baking soda
1 teaspoon ground cinnamon
1 teaspoon ground nutmeg
1/4 teaspoon ground allspice
1/4 teaspoon ground cloves
1/4 cup milk
1 cup chopped nuts

In a saucepan, combine molasses, water and vanilla; add raisins and bring to a boil. Reduce heat and simmer for 5 minutes. Remove from heat and stir in fruit; cool. Meanwhile, in a mixing bowl, cream butter and sugar. Add the eggs, one at a time, beating well after each addition. Stir together dry ingredients; add to creamed mixture alternately with milk. Stir in fruit mixture; mix well. Fold in nuts. Spoon into paper-lined miniature muffin tins, filling almost to the top. Bake at 325° for 22-24 minutes or until cakes test done. Cool on wire racks. Store in airtight containers. **Yield:** about 6 dozen.

HOLLY WREATHS

Dee Lien, Longmont, Colorado

(PICTURED ON PAGE 86)

1 cup butter, softened
1 package (3 ounces) cream cheese, softened
1/2 cup sugar
1 teaspoon vanilla extract
2 cups all-purpose flour
Green cherries, cut into thin slices
Cinnamon red-hot candies
Frosting and decorator gel

In a mixing bowl, cream butter and cream cheese. Add sugar; blend well. Stir in vanilla. Gradually beat in flour. Using a cookie press fitted with star tip, form dough into 2-1/2-in. wreaths on ungreased baking sheets. Bake at 375° for 10-12 minutes or until set but not brown. Cool on wire racks. Decorate wreaths with green cherry "leaves" and cinnamon candy "berries" attached with a drop of frosting. Add bows with decorator gel. **Yield:** about 3 dozen.

HAYSTACKS

Starrlette Howard, Ogden, Utah

1 package (6 ounces) butterscotch chips
1/2 cup peanut butter
1 can (3 ounces) chow mein noodles
1 cup miniature marshmallows

Melt butterscotch chips and peanut butter in the top of a double boiler. Fold in the chow mein noodles, then marshmallows. Drop by teaspoonfuls onto greased waxed paper. Cool. **Yield:** 2 dozen.

MAPLE-GLAZED APPLE PIE

Patricia Putnam, Lakeland, Florida

(PICTURED ON PAGE 88)

Pastry for double-crust pie (9 inches)
6 cups thinly sliced peeled apples, *divided*
1/2 cup sugar
1/4 cup packed brown sugar
1/2 cup crushed gingersnaps
1/2 teaspoon ground cinnamon
1/2 cup chopped walnuts *or* pecans
1/4 cup butter *or* margarine, melted
1/4 cup maple syrup

Line a 9-in. pie pan with the bottom crust. Place half of the apples in the crust; set aside. In a mixing bowl, combine sugars, gingersnaps, cinnamon, nuts and butter; sprinkle half over apples in crust. Top with remaining apples and sugar mixture. Roll out remaining pastry to fit top of pie. Cut a few slits in the top and place over apples; seal. Cover loosely with foil and bake at 375° for 35 minutes. Meanwhile, bring syrup to a gentle boil in a small saucepan. Remove pie from oven; remove foil and brush hot syrup over pie and into vents. Return pie to oven and bake, uncovered, 20 minutes longer. Serve warm. **Yield:** 8 servings.

CORNISH HENS WITH WILD RICE

Evelyn Panka, Canby, Minnesota

(PICTURED ON PAGE 88)

1 can (10-3/4 ounces)
  condensed cream of
  mushroom soup, undiluted
2/3 cup milk
1 cup (4 ounces) shredded
  cheddar cheese
3 slices bacon
1 cup finely chopped onion
1/2 cup chopped green pepper
4-1/2 cups cooked wild rice
1 cup all-purpose flour
1 teaspoon salt
1/2 teaspoon paprika
1/4 teaspoon pepper
3 Cornish game hens, halved
4 tablespoons shortening
Finely chopped parsley

In a saucepan, combine soup and milk. Cook over medium heat until smooth; stir in cheese. Meanwhile, in a skillet, fry bacon until crisp. Remove bacon; crumble and set aside. In drippings, saute onion and green pepper until tender. Add to soup mixture along with wild rice; mix well. Pour into a greased 15-in. x 10-in. x 2-in. baking dish; top with bacon. Combine flour, salt, paprika and pepper in a heavy plastic bag; place one or two hens at a time in bag and shake to coat well. In another skillet, melt shortening. Brown hens on all sides. Arrange on top of rice mixture. Bake, uncovered, at 350° for 45 minutes or until meat is tender. Sprinkle with parsley. **Yield:** 6 servings.

FROZEN CRANBERRY SALAD

Beverly Mix, Missoula, Montana

(PICTURED ON PAGE 88)

4 packages (3 ounces each)
  cream cheese, softened
1/4 cup salad dressing or
  mayonnaise
2 tablespoons sugar
1 carton (16 ounces) frozen
  whipped topping, thawed
2 cans (20 ounces each)
  crushed pineapple, drained
2 cups chopped walnuts
2 cups flaked coconut
2 cans (16 ounces each)
  whole-berry cranberry sauce
1 cup fresh or frozen
  cranberries, chopped, optional
Lettuce leaves

In a medium bowl, blend cream cheese, salad dressing and sugar. Fold in the whipped topping; set aside. In a large mixing bowl, combine pineapple, nuts, coconut and cranberry sauce. Add cranberries if desired. Gently combine with cream cheese mixture. Spread into a 13-in. x 9-in. x 2-in. glass baking dish or three foil-lined 8-in. x 4-in. x 2-in. loaf pans. Cover and freeze. Remove from freezer 10-15 minutes before serving. Cut into squares or slices. Serve on lettuce leaves. **Yield:** 24 servings.

TWICE-BAKED POTATOES

Debbie Jones, California, Maryland

6 large baking potatoes
1/2 cup butter or margarine,
  softened
3/4 to 1 cup milk or cream
3 tablespoons crumbled
  cooked bacon
3 tablespoons minced onion
1 tablespoon snipped chives
1/2 teaspoon salt
Dash pepper
1-1/2 cups (6 ounces) shredded
  cheddar cheese, *divided*
Paprika

Bake potatoes at 400° for 60 minutes or until soft. Cut a lengthwise slice from the top of the potatoes. Scoop out the pulp and place in a bowl. Mash potatoes and butter. Blend in milk or cream, bacon, onion, chives, salt, pepper and 1 cup of cheese. Refill potato shells. Top with remaining cheese and sprinkle with paprika. Bake at 375° for 25-30 minutes or until heated through. **Yield:** 6 servings.

STUFFED BEEF TENDERLOIN

Norma Blank, Shawano, Wisconsin

1/4 cup butter or margarine
1 medium onion, chopped
1/2 cup diced celery
1 can (4 ounces) chopped
  mushrooms, drained
2 cups soft bread crumbs
  (about 3 slices)
1/2 to 1 teaspoon salt
1/8 teaspoon pepper
1/4 teaspoon dried basil or 1
  teaspoon fresh basil
1/4 teaspoon dried parsley flakes
  or 1 teaspoon chopped fresh
  parsley

1 beef tenderloin (about 3
  pounds), trimmed
4 slices bacon

In a small skillet, melt butter over low heat. Saute onion, celery and mushrooms until onion is soft and transparent. Meanwhile, in a mixing bowl, combine bread crumbs, salt, pepper, basil and parsley. Add onion mixture and mix well. Make a lengthwise cut 3/4 of the way through the tenderloin. Lightly place stuffing in the pocket; close with toothpicks. Place bacon strips diagonally across the top, covering the picks and pocket. Place meat, bacon side up, in a shallow roasting pan. Insert meat thermometer into meat, not stuffing. Bake, uncovered, at 350° until meat reaches desired degree of doneness: 140° for rare, 160° for medium and 170° for well-done. (Meat will need to bake approximately 1 hour for medium.) Remove from oven; let stand for 15 minutes. Remove toothpicks and slice. **Yield:** 10-12 servings.

WILD RICE SOUP

Miriam Yarish, Rice Lake, Wisconsin

1 large meaty ham bone
1 large onion, chopped
Water
1-1/2 cups uncooked wild rice,
  rinsed and drained
6 tablespoons butter or
  margarine
6 tablespoons all-purpose flour
2 cups heavy cream
3 egg yolks
3 jars (4-1/2 ounces each)
  sliced mushrooms
1 can (14-1/2 ounces) chicken
  broth
1/2 teaspoon white pepper
1 teaspoon dried thyme
1 tablespoon chopped parsley
Milk

Place ham bone, onion and 3 qts. water in an 8-qt. soup kettle or Dutch oven; simmer for 2-1/2 hours. Remove ham bone. When cool enough to handle, remove meat from the bone; set aside. Discard bone. Add wild rice to stock. Simmer for 1 more hour or until tender. Remove from heat; drain and reserve stock. Set rice and onion aside. Add enough water to stock to make 2 qts.; set aside. In the same kettle, melt butter. Stir in flour and cook over medium heat for 2 minutes. Do not brown. Gradually stir in reserved stock. Bring to a rapid boil over high heat; boil for 3 minutes, stirring constantly. Remove from the heat. In a mixing bowl, combine cream and yolks. Add 1 cup stock to egg mixture, then stir into kettle. Return soup to heat; heat gently over medium-low. Do not boil. Add reserved rice, onion and ham along with mushrooms, chicken broth, pepper, thyme and parsley. Thin with milk if necessary. **Yield:** 12-16 servings (4 quarts).

SPICED PECANS

Brenda Schneider, Armington, Illinois

1/2 cup sugar
1 tablespoon ground cinnamon
1/2 teaspoon salt
1 egg white
1 pound large pecan halves

Combine sugar, cinnamon and salt in a small bowl; set aside. In a large mixing bowl, lightly beat egg white. Add pecans; stir until coated. Sprinkle sugar mixture over pecans; mix well. Spread in a single layer on a baking sheet. Bake at 300° for 20 minutes. Remove nuts from baking sheet while warm to cool on waxed paper. **Yield:** about 6 cups.

KIPPLENS

Susan Bohannon, Kokomo, Indiana

2 cups butter *or* margarine
1 cup sugar
5 cups all-purpose flour
2 teaspoons vanilla extract
2 cups chopped pecans
1/4 teaspoon salt
Confectioners' sugar

In a mixing bowl, cream butter and sugar; add flour, vanilla, pecans and salt. Mix well. Roll dough into 1-in. balls and place on ungreased cookie sheets. Bake at 325° for 17-20 minutes or until lightly browned. Cool cookies slightly before rolling them in confectioners' sugar. **Yield:** 12 dozen.

LEMON-BUTTER SPRITZ COOKIES

Paula Pelis, Rocky Point, New York

2 cups butter (no substitutes)
1-1/4 cups sugar
2 eggs
Grated peel of 1 lemon
2 teaspoons lemon juice
1 teaspoon vanilla extract
5-1/4 cups all-purpose flour
1/4 teaspoon salt
Colored sugar

In a large mixing bowl, cream butter and sugar. Add the eggs, lemon peel, lemon juice and vanilla; mix well. Stir together flour and salt; gradually add to creamed mixture. Using a cookie press, shape into designs on ungreased cookie sheets. Sprinkle with colored sugar. Bake at 400° for 8-10 minutes or until lightly brown around the edges. **Yield:** about 12 dozen.

CHERRY/PEAR MINCEMEAT

Brenda Wood, Egbert, Ontario

6 cups pitted tart red cherries
6 cups ripe pears, cored and coarsely chopped
2 pounds raisins
1 lemon, juiced
1 orange, juiced
Grated peel of lemon
Grated peel of orange
5 cups sugar
3/4 cup vinegar
3/4 cup apple juice
2 teaspoons ground cinnamon
2 teaspoons ground nutmeg
2 teaspoons ground allspice
2 teaspoons ground ginger
1 teaspoon ground cloves

In a large kettle, combine all ingredients. Bring to a boil. Reduce heat and simmer, uncovered, until mixture thickens, about 2-1/2 to 3 hours. Stir frequently while simmering. Chill. **Yield:** about 3 quarts.

SOUR CREAM TWISTS

Kathy Floyd, Greenville, Florida

1 package (1/4 ounce) active dry yeast
1/4 cup warm water (110°-115°)
4 cups all-purpose flour
3/4 teaspoon salt
1/2 cup butter *or* margarine
1/2 cup shortening
2 eggs, lightly beaten
1/2 cup sour cream
3 teaspoons vanilla extract, *divided*
1-1/2 cups sugar
Red *or* green colored sugar

In a small bowl, dissolve yeast in water. Let stand 5 minutes. In a mixing bowl, stir together flour and salt. Cut in butter and shortening until particles are the size of small peas. Stir in eggs, sour cream, 1 teaspoon vanilla and the yeast mixture. Mix thoroughly (dough will be stiff and resemble pie pastry).

Combine white sugar and remaining vanilla; lightly sprinkle 1/2 cup over a pastry cloth. Roll out half of the dough into a rectangle. Sprinkle with about 1 tablespoon of the sugar mixture plus some red or green colored sugar. Fold rectangle into thirds (fold one end of dough over center and fold other end over to make three layers). Give dough a quarter turn and repeat rolling, sugaring and folding two more times. Roll out into a 16-in. x 9-in. rectangle. Cut into 3-in. x 1-in. strips. Twist each strip two or three times. Place on chilled ungreased baking sheets. Repeat with remaining dough, sugar mixture and colored sugar. Bake at 375° for 15-20 minutes or until light golden brown. Immediately remove cookies to wire racks. **Yield:** 8 dozen.

TURKEY LEGS WITH MUSHROOM GRAVY

Wanda Swenson, Lady Lake, Florida

 This tasty dish uses less sugar, salt and fat. Recipe includes *Diabetic Exchanges*.

4 turkey legs (about 12 ounces *each*)
1/4 cup lemon juice
2 tablespoons cooking oil
1 teaspoon dried oregano
1 teaspoon dried basil
1 teaspoon garlic powder
1/4 teaspoon salt
1/4 teaspoon pepper
MUSHROOM GRAVY:
1 cup water
1 tablespoon cornstarch
1 can (4 ounces) sliced mushrooms, drained
1 can (10-1/2 ounces) mushroom gravy
1 teaspoon minced onion
1 tablespoon minced fresh parsley
1 teaspoon garlic powder

Place turkey legs in a roasting pan. In a small bowl, combine lemon juice, oil and seasonings. Pour over turkey legs. Bake, uncovered, at 375° for 45 minutes or until lightly browned. Turn legs twice and baste occasionally. Remove from the oven. For the gravy, combine water and cornstarch in a saucepan. Stir in remaining ingredients and bring to a boil over medium heat. Spoon over turkey legs. Cover loosely with foil. Bake, basting frequently, for 1 hour or until legs are tender. **Yield:** 4 servings. **Diabetic Exchanges:** One serving equals 4 lean meat, 1-1/2 fat, 1 vegetable, 1/2 starch; also, 357 calories, 703 mg sodium, 97 mg cholesterol, 11 gm carbohydrate, 36 gm protein, 18 gm fat.

'My Most Memorable Meal'

Holidays during the '30's always brought relatives from near and far to Patricia Baxter's childhood home.

"I'll never forget my cousins constantly slipping into the kitchen to snitch samples of Mother's goodies as she prepared them," says Patricia, who lives in Great Bend, Kansas. "When dinner was finally announced, Mother should have been exhausted, but instead she seemed fresh, satisfied and content. Her huge dinner was always a masterpiece."

Patricia's "Most Memorable Meal" starred roast turkey, and also featured the four dishes presented here. But, Patricia adds, "Most important was the love that Mother put into those feasts—it seemed to fill our home along with the aromas."

'TIS THE SEASON. Clockwise from top left: **Mother's Rolls, Raisin Pie, Cauliflower with Almonds, Molded Cranberry Salad** (all recipes on page 95).

MOTHER'S ROLLS

- 2 packages (1/4 ounce *each*) active dry yeast
- 1 cup warm water (110°-115°)
- 1/3 cup sugar
- 2 teaspoons salt
- 1/3 cup shortening, melted and cooled
- 1 egg, beaten
- 1-1/2 cups warm milk (110°-115°)
- 7 to 7-1/2 cups all-purpose flour

In a large mixing bowl, dissolve yeast in water. Add sugar, salt, shortening, egg, milk and 3 cups flour. Stir until mixture has a spongy texture. Let rest for 10 minutes. Mix in enough of the remaining flour to form a soft dough. Turn out onto a lightly floured board; knead until smooth and elastic, about 8-10 minutes. Place in a greased bowl, turning once to grease top. Cover and let rise until doubled, about 1 hour. Punch dough down. Turn out onto a lightly floured surface and divide in thirds. Let rest for 5 minutes. Grease 36 muffin cups. Divide each third of dough into 36 pieces. Shape each piece into a ball, pulling edges under to make a smooth surface. Arrange three balls, smooth side up, in each muffin cup. Cover and let rise until almost doubled, about 30 minutes. Bake at 375° for 12-15 minutes or until golden brown. **Yield:** 3 dozen. *If cooking for two:* Freeze rolls in a plastic storage bag. Then defrost as many as needed at a moment's notice.

RAISIN PIE

- 1 cup sugar
- 2-1/2 tablespoons all-purpose flour
- 1-1/2 cups cold water
- 2 cups raisins
- 1/2 teaspoon salt
- 1/2 teaspoon ground cinnamon
- 1 tablespoon butter *or* margarine
- Pastry for double-crust pie (9 inches)

In a saucepan, stir together sugar and flour. Add water and mix well. Stir in raisins, salt and cinnamon; cook and stir over medium heat until bubbly. Cook and stir 1 minute more. Remove from heat and stir in butter. Pour into a pastry-lined pie plate. Top with lattice crust, or cover with top crust and cut slits for steam to escape. Bake at 375° for about 45 minutes or until crust is golden brown. **Yield:** 6-8 servings.

CAULIFLOWER WITH ALMONDS

- 1 medium head cauliflower (about 1-1/2 pounds)
- 2 tablespoons butter *or* margarine
- 2 tablespoons all-purpose flour
- 1/4 teaspoon salt
- 1 cup milk
- Shredded cheddar cheese
- 2 tablespoons sliced almonds, toasted
- Paprika
- Cooked green beans, optional

Trim leaves from cauliflower, leaving 1 in. of stem for support. Place in Dutch oven; add hot water that covers stem but does not touch head. Cover and steam until tender, about 12-15 minutes. Meanwhile, melt butter in a small saucepan; blend in flour and salt. Add milk. Cook and stir over medium heat until thickened and bubbly; cook and stir 1 minute longer. To serve, cut off stem and place cauliflower on a serving dish. Spoon the sauce over and sprinkle with cheese, almonds and paprika. Accompany with green beans if desired. **Yield:** 6-8 servings.

MOLDED CRANBERRY SALAD

- 8 cups fresh cranberries
- 2-1/2 cups sugar
- 2 tablespoons unflavored gelatin
- 1/3 cup orange juice
- 2 cups diced apples
- 1 cup chopped nuts
- Leaf lettuce and mayonnaise for garnish

Finely grind the cranberries in a food chopper. Add sugar and mix thoroughly. Let stand 15 minutes, stirring occasionally. (If using frozen berries, let them stand until the mixture is at room temperature.) Place the gelatin and orange juice in the top of a double boiler; stir over hot water until gelatin is dissolved. Add to cranberries along with apples and nuts; place in a 7-cup mold that has been rinsed in cold water. Chill until set. Unmold onto leaf lettuce. Garnish with mayonnaise. **Yield:** 12 servings.

LITTLE GIRL PIES

Pat Nofsinger, Charlotte, North Carolina

- 1 cup sugar
- 1/2 cup shortening
- 1 egg
- 1/2 cup milk
- 1 teaspoon vanilla extract
- 3-1/2 cups all-purpose flour
- 1/2 teaspoon salt
- 4 teaspoons baking powder

FILLING:
- 1/2 cup sugar
- 1 tablespoon cornstarch
- 1/2 cup water
- 1 cup raisins

In a mixing bowl, cream sugar and shortening. Add egg, milk and vanilla; mix well. Combine dry ingredients; add to creamed mixture and beat well. Chill. Meanwhile, for filling, combine sugar and cornstarch in a saucepan. Add water; stir to dissolve. Add raisins; cook and stir until mixture comes to a boil and thickens, about 3 minutes. Set aside to cool. Divide chilled dough into thirds. Roll one-third out on a lightly floured board to 1/8-in. thickness. Cut into 3-in. circles. Using a thimble, cut small holes in the center of half of the circles. Place 1 teaspoon filling on solid circles; top each with a circle that has a hole. Pinch edges together to seal. Repeat with remaining dough and filling. Bake on ungreased cookie sheets at 375° for 15-17 minutes or until lightly browned. **Yield:** 2 dozen cookies.

SWEET POTATOES FOR TWO

Flo Burtnett, Gage, Oklahoma

- 2 to 3 sweet potatoes, cooked and peeled
- 1/2 cup packed brown sugar
- 2 tablespoons butter *or* margarine
- 2 tablespoons water
- 1/4 teaspoon salt
- Dash ground nutmeg *or* ground mace

Slice sweet potatoes into an 8-in. pie plate; set aside. In a saucepan, combine brown sugar, butter, water and salt; bring to a boil. Pour hot syrup over potatoes. Bake, uncovered, at 350° for 30 minutes, basting occasionally, or until syrup thickens and potatoes are glazed. Sprinkle with nutmeg or mace. **Yield:** 2 servings.

D

F

G